SCOTTISH
LAND LAW

SUPPLEMENT I
TO
VOLUME I

SCOTTISH LAND LAW

SUPPLEMENT I
TO
VOLUME I

by

William M Gordon
MA, LLB, PhD, LLD (Hon), FRSE
former Professor of Civil Law
at the University of Glasgow

Published under the auspices of
SCOTTISH UNIVERSITIES LAW INSTITUTE LTD

W. GREEN  **THOMSON REUTERS**

Published in 2011 by
W. Green, 21 Alva Street, Edinburgh EH2 4PS
Part of Thomson Reuters (Professional) UK Limited
(Registered in England and Wales, Company No 1679046
Registered office and address for service:
Aldgate House,
33 Aldgate High Street, London EC3N 1DL)

http://www.wgreen.thomson.com

Typeset by Keith Thaxton at W. Green, Edinburgh
Printed and bound in Great Britain by Ashford Colour Press, Gosport, Hants

A catalogue record for this title is available from the British Library

ISBN 978-0-414-01867-9

A catalogue record for this title is available
from the British Library

No natural forests were destroyed to make this product;
only farmed timber was used and replanted

CONTENTS

The **Supplement** is arranged in the order of the Prelims and paragraphs of Volume 1.

TABLE OF CASES

TABLE OF STATUTES

TABLE OF STATUTORY INSTRUMENTS

TABLE OF EUROPEAN LEGISLATION

Directives

ABBREVIATIONS

Crawford, *International* E.B. Crawford and J M. Carruthers,
Private Law International Private Law—A Scots Perspective, 3rd edn
(W. Green, 2010).

ERRATA

p.xxvii *Compugraphics International Ltd v Nicolic*—delete 1–54
p.xcvii Crofters (Scotland) Act 1993 ss.38–39—"18–184"
p.civ Water Environment and Water Services (Scotland) Act 2003 s.20—6–42
s.22—6–42
p.cxxiii Water Services etc—"(SI 2005/3172)"
p.cxxiv Scotland Act 1998—"(SI 2006/2913)"
p.441 Heading THE LAW OF THE TENEMENT (12)—delete "sues"
p.557 fn.41—second last line—"Accreditation".
p.670—Index—Under **Judicial Factors** add "15–18, 16–01"
12–11 fn.35. The reference to *Conveyancing 2008* should be to pp.133 et seq.
fn.36. Professor Rennie should appear as the fourth professor of conveyancing
in place of Professor Gretton who is inadvertently mentioned twice.

fn.16. *Baron of Ardgowan v Lord Lyon, King of Arms*, reversed [2009] CSIH   **1–03**
61; 2009 S.L.T. 759; *sub nom. Kerr v Advocate General*, 2010 S.C. 1. holding
that the Lord Lyon was entitled to require a substantial territorial connection
before registering a name indicating a territorial connection and to decide that
a bare superiority title was insufficient.

For general information see the websites of the Convention of the
Baronage of Scotland, *http://www.scotsbarons.org* [accessed August 15,
2011] and the Heraldry Society of Scotland, *http://www.heraldry-
scotland.co.uk* [accessed August 15, 2011].

fn.117. The 2008 Regulations are amended by the Protected Trust Deeds   **1–49**
(Scotland) Amendment Regulations 2010 (SSI 2010/398) to deal with
secured creditors who have consented to their exclusion.

For a general treatise on jurisdiction see G. Maher and B.J. Rodger, *Civil*   **1–52**
Jurisdiction in the Scottish Courts (W. Green, 2010). In relation to heritable
property a third edition of A.E Anton and P.R. Beaumont, *Private*
International Law (W. Green, 2011) is due.

There are relatively minor amendments to the references to Crawford,   **1–56 and**
International Private Law. Property is still dealt with in Ch.17 and the most   **1–57**
relevant paras are 17–02 to 17–10; succession is still dealt with in Ch.18 and
the most relevant paras are 18–12 to 18–27, with a discussion of European
proposals for harmonisation of the law which would affect the distinction
between moveable and immoveable property at paras 18–35 et seq; contract
is still dealt with in Ch.15 and the most relevant paras are 15–16 et seq and
15–36 to 15–38.

3–02 See D.A. Nisbet, "Worlds Apart" (2010) 55(5) J.L.S. 52 on relevant websites.

3–07 *Clydesdale Homes Ltd v Quay* [2009] CSOH 126; 2009 G.W.D 31-518, noted in 2009 Prop. L.B. 103-18. Once a title has been registered the plan registered becomes definitive of the boundaries but problems may still arise because of the scale of the plan which makes it impossible to show small features exactly. See also *Welsh v Keeper of the Registers of Scotland*, 2010 G.W.D. 23-443, Lands Tr. and discussions in *Conveyancing 2009*, pp.173–177 and *Conveyancing 2010*, pp.158–159.

3–13 **fn.57.** *Compugraphics International Ltd v Nicolic* reversed on this point on appeal [2011] CSIH 34; 2011 G.W.D. 17-414; 2011 S.C.L.R. 481.

3–52 **fn.205.** See for the results of the latest consultation on possible remedies for nuisance hedges the Scottish Government website s.v. High hedges. A Member's Bill is expected to be introduced in 2011.

fn.28. In *Post Office Ltd v Assessor for Renfrewshire Valuation Joint Board* **4–06**
[2010] CSIH 93 the parties agreed that an ATM machine bolted to the floor
inside a post office, with access from outside, was not a fixture; cf. also
Assessor for Central Scotland Joint Valuation Board v Bank of Ireland
[2010] CSIH 91; 2011 S.L.T. 369; 2011 S.C. 265.

5–15   **fn.42.** See also M. Alramahi, J. Karlberg and L. Moller, *Oil and Gas Law in the UK* (Bloomsbury Professional, 2011).

5–23   Part II of the Coast Protection Act 1949, dealing with the restriction of works detrimental to navigation, is repealed for Scotland by the Marine (Scotland) Act 2010 Sch.4, Pt 1 para.1, being replaced by the more general provisions of the Marine and Coastal Access Act 2009 and the 2010 Act. The 2009 Act repeals it for England and Wales.

5–32   **fn.104.** The decision is affirmed for somewhat different reasons *sub nom. The Scottish Coal Co Ltd v Danish Forestry Co Ltd* [2010] CSIH 56; 2010 S.C. 729; *Conveyancing 2010*, pp.110–112.

5–54   The issue whether a reservation of minerals might include material deposited
and 5–55   as well as unworked minerals was raised in *Braes v Keeper of the Registers of Scotland* [2009] CSOH 176; 2010 S.L.T. 689; G. Junor, "Pre-emptions, Promises and Prospective Liabilities", 2010 S.L.T. (News) 95 at 97. Reference was made to Rennie, *Minerals*, paras 2.11–2.14.

5–67   **fn.182.** *G. Hamilton (Tullochgribban Mains) Ltd v The Highland Council* [2011] CSIH 1; 2011 S.C. 361.

fn.184. Part II of the Environmental Impact Assessment (Scotland) Regulations 1999 (SSI 199/1), as amended, is replaced by the consolidating and updated Town and Country Planning (Environmental Impact Assessment) (Scotland) Regulations 2011 (SSI 2011/139).

On the Crown's rights in the sea-bed see *Crown Estate Comrs, Petitioners* **6–02**
[2010] CSOH 70; 2010 S.L.T. 741.

See the note on para.**5–23** above. **6–04**

The Scottish Government's legislative programme for 2011–2012 includes a **6–41 et**
Water Bill which will deal with a strategy to maximise water resources, the **seq.**
powers of Scottish Water to develop its assets, the management of the water
environment, drought orders, control of substances in the water environment
and the management of septic tanks, thus affecting these paras and paras **6–72**
and **6–73**, **6–74 et seq**, **6–78** and **6–79**.

The Water Environment (Controlled Activities) (Scotland) Regulations 2011 **6–41**
(SSI 2011/209) replace the 2005 Regulations (SSI 2005/348) which are
revoked, along with amending provisions detailed in reg.58, in the light of the
consolidation and amendment brought about by the 2011 Regulations. These
essentially maintain the scheme of the 2005 Regulations but update it.

fn.138. The amending provisions in the 2011 Regulations revoke SSIs 2006/
553, 2007/219 and 2008/54.
    Water Environment and Water Services (Scotland) Act 2003
(Consequential Provisions and Modifications) Order 2006 (SI 2006/1054).

fn.143. Water Environment (Groundwater and Priority Substances) **6–42**
(Scotland) Regulations 2009 (SSI 2009/420); reg.4 and Schs 1 and 2 are
revoked by the Controlled Activities Regulations 2011, reg.58(e).

fn.152. S. Hendry, "Water Resources Management: Current Developments"
(2009) 134 S.P.E.L. 87 and "River Basin Plans, Classifications and Standards
Directions" (2010) 139 S.P.E.L. 63.

fn.158. The Reservoirs (Scotland) Act 2011, s.109 amends the 2003 Act s.22(3)
to add para.3(c) giving further powers to make regulations and adds Sch.2A on
offences under the regulations.

fn.165. Water Industry (Scotland) Act 2002 (Consequential Modifications) **6–43**
Order 2004 (SI 2004/1822), replacing references to water authority with
Scottish Water.

See para.**6–41** above on the new Controlled Activities Regulations. **6–49**

On issues arising in setting up hydro-electric schemes see A. Scott, "Mini **6–60**
Hydro Schemes", 2010 Prop. L.B. 108-6.

fn.251. *Anderson v Shetland Council* [2010] CSIH 15; 2010 S.C. 446—case **6–62**
based on omission to discharge statutory duties on drainage, sewerage and
roads dismissed as irrelevant but indicating that a common law action might
be possible.

The Flood Risk Management Act 2009 (asp 6), noted by T. Bell in (2009) 133 **6–64**
S.P.E.L. 54 and 134 S.P.E.L. 93, was brought partially into force by the Flood

Risk Management (Scotland) Act 2009 (Commencement No.1 and Transitional and Savings Provisions) Order 2009 (SSI 2009/393) bringing most of it into force from November 26, 2009, except Pts 4 and 7 and the sections of Pt 6 relating to local authorities; the 1st Annual Report to Parliament, May 13, 2010 indicated that a further commencement order in 2010 would bring Pt 4 and the rest of Pt 6 into force. Part 7 will be repealed by the Reservoirs (Scotland) Act 2011 (asp 9) s.112.

The Flood Risk Management (Scotland) Act 2009 (Commencement No.2 and Savings Provisions) Order 2010 (SSI 2010/401) then brought s.60 and Sch.2, paras 13 and 14 into force from November 29, 2010; most of the remainder of Pt 4 (except ss.62–64 on registers of flood protection schemes) with relevant sections in Pt 6, together with the remainder of Sch.2 and Sch.3, came into force from December 24, 2010 and ss.59 and 79(2)(h) into force from June 1, 2011. The savings relate to flood prevention schemes put in train under the Flood Prevention (Scotland) Act 1961, which is repealed by s.70.

The Flood Risk Management (Flood Protection Schemes, Potentially Vulnerable Areas and Local Plan Districts) (Scotland) Regulations 2010 (SSI 2010/426) made under ss.15, 60(2)(b) and Sch.2, paras 13 and 14 and in force from December 24, 2010, provide for the documentation required in identification of potentially vulnerable areas and local plan districts, environmental impact assessments and procedure in connection with these and flood protection schemes.

On January 18, 2011 a consultation was launched on the proposed statutory guidance to be issued under ss.2(5) and 29 of the Act to SEPA, local authorities and Scottish Water on the fulfilment of their responsibilities under the Act to provide a sustainable and collaborative approach to managing flood risk. The guidance was intended to be issued in May and the consultation paper contains a time-table for implementation of the provisions of the Act.

6–75   Under the Public Services Reform (Scotland) Act 2010 (asp 8) s.3, brought into force, along with ss.130 and 131 and Schs 2 and 3, from August 15, 2011 by the fifth Commencement Order (SSI 2011/278), the National Consumer Council takes over from the Water Customer Consultation Panels which are dissolved, as is Waterwatch Scotland.

fn.327. The Provision of Water and Sewerage Services (Reasonable Cost) (Scotland) Regulations 2011 (SSI 2011/119) replace and revoke the 2006 Regulations.

fn.328. The Water Quality (Scotland) Regulations 2010 (SSI 2010/95) further transpose Council Directive 98/83/EC, the Drinking Water Directive, in response to an infraction case and a reasoned opinion of the EC that it had not been transposed correctly.

fn.331. See now the Natural Water, Spring Water and Bottled Drinking Water (Scotland) Amendment Regulations 2009 (SSI 2009/273) as further amended by SSI 2010/89, SSI 2010/127 and SSI 2011/94.

fn.335. The Water Services Charges (Billing and Collection) (Scotland) Order 2010 (SSI 2010/10) replaces the 2006 Order.

6–81 and   The Flood Risk Management (Scotland) Act 2009, Pt 7, making SEPA the
6–82   enforcement authority under the Reservoirs Act 1975 and making other

amendments of the 1975 Act is still not in force and is to be repealed by the Reservoirs (Scotland) Bill 2010 which was given the Royal Assent on April 12, 2011 as the Reservoirs (Scotland) Act 2011 (asp 9). The Act will provide a new scheme for control of reservoirs, for which scheme SEPA will have ultimate responsibility. The Reservoirs Act 1975 will be repealed (2011 Act, s.8) and replaced by provisions which in general affect reservoirs holding 10,000 cubic metres of water above the level of the surrounding land, along with associated structures, subject to modification by order made by the Scottish Ministers. These reservoirs are described as controlled reservoirs and require a reservoir manager (ss.1–7). Controlled reservoirs will require to be registered by SEPA (ss.9–17) which will give each a risk designation as high-risk, medium-risk or low-risk, having regard to the risks of damage by the uncontrolled release of the water they contain (s.22) (ss.18–26). A panel of reservoir engineers is to be created (ss.27–31, expanded by regulations) and there will be controls over construction, alteration and management of the reservoirs affected, with the most stringent controls affecting high- and medium-risk reservoirs (ss.45–53), all with a view to reducing the risk of flooding. Other requirements affecting all controlled reservoirs are incident reports (s.54 and regulations), flood plans (s.55, with regulations), record-keeping (s.56 and regulations) and display of emergency response information (s.57).

There is provision for referral by reservoir managers of disputes over safety and inspection reports and certificates required by various provisions of the Act (ss.59–64, with regulations). There is very elaborate provision for civil enforcement of obligations imposed by the Act, including enforcement notices issued by SEPA (ss.65–70) with power to step in (s.71), extended remedies available to a court (s.72), stop notices (ss.73–77), undertakings (s.78), fixed penalties (ss.79–81), further measures introduced by order made by the Scottish Ministers (ss.82–84) and non-compliance penalties (s.85), all additional to the criminal penalties for the various offences created. Consultation will be required before using the powers in ss.73(1), 78(1), 79(1) and 82(1) and guidance is to be issued on use of the various civil remedies and appeals (ss.87 and 89). Enforcement action may be publicised (s.90) and there is provision for entry on land, by warrant if necessary, with compensation for damage caused (ss.91–95).

SEPA is to report to the Scottish Ministers on compliance with the Act, getting guidance from them on the operation of Pt 1 of the Act (ss.1–108) and being entitled to obtain information and assistance (ss.96, 98 and 100). There are various supplementary provisions on such matters as Crown application, offences by corporate bodies, amendments and repeals and a list of defined expressions and a provision that there is no civil liability for damages for breach of obligations imposed by the Act (s.108) (ss.100–108, 110–116). At present only ss.1, 2, 7, 114 (orders and regulations), 115 (defined expressions) and 116 (short title and commencement) are in force.

See the note on para.**5–23** above. **6–99**

7–12 **fn.43.** St Andrews Harbour Revision (Constitution) Order 2010 (SSI 2010/403); Caledonian Maritime Assets (Port Ellen) Harbour Revision Order 2011 (SSI 2011/283); Scrabster (Deep Inner Berth) Harbour Revision Order 2011 (SS. 2011/284); Ullapool Harbour Revision (Constitution) Order 2011 (SSI 2011/338).

fn.44. Loch Ryan Port (Harbour Empowerment) Order 2009 (SSI 2010/31).

7–15 **fn.55.** *Crown Estate Comrs, Petitioners* [2010] CSOH 70; 2010 S.L.T. 74—a grant of port and harbour does not entitle individuals to lay moorings on the sea-bed.

7–34 **fn.120.** See also the Scottish Government publication *Treasure Trove in Scotland: A Code of Practice* (2008) and references to treasure trove in the SLC *Discussion Paper on Prescription and Title to Moveable Property* (D.P. No.144, December 2010).

7–37 **fn.129.** See the SLC Discussion Paper (para.**7–34** above), Pt. 9.

7–41 **fn.145.** The Protection of Wrecks Act 1973 is to be repealed by the Marine (Scotland) Act 2010 (asp 5) Sch.4, Pt 2 para.4 in the light of the provisions on marine protection and enhancement in Pt 5 of the 2010 Act, which in s.67(1)(c) and s.73 envisage the creation of historic marine protection areas.

The Scottish Government's legislative programme for 2011–2012 includes an **8–02 et** Aquaculture and Fisheries Bill dealing with the management of farmed fish **seq.** and wild salmon and freshwater fisheries, the amendment and updating of sea fisheries legislation and the continued protection of shellfish growing waters and so is liable to affect these paragraphs and paras **8–24 et seq**, **8–87 et seq**, **8–145 et seq** and **8–153 et seq**.

The Sea Fish (Conservation) Act 1967 is modified by the Marine and Coastal **8–13** Access Act 2009 Pt 7, Ch.1 (ss.194–201) and Schs 15 and 22 and these modifications apply to Scotland with exceptions set out in the Marine (Scotland) Act 2010 s.158, while s.22A, applying the 1967 Act to Scotland, is modified by s.159. The relevant provisions of the 2010 Act were brought into force as from February 24, 2011 by the Marine (Scotland) Act (Commencement No.2 and Transitional Provisions) Order 2011 (SSI 2011/58) ("the Second Commencement Order") art.2.

The Aquaculture and Fisheries (Scotland) Act 2007 (Fixed Penalty Notices) Amendment Order 2011 (SSI 2011/60) amends the 2008 Order (SSI 2008/101), revokes other provisions and substitutes a new Sch.1 to the 2008 Order.

fn.22. The Inshore Fishing (Prohibition of Fishing for Cockles) (Solway Firth) (Scotland) Order 2011 (SSI 2011/319).

Part 6 (ss.107–130) of the Marine (Scotland) Act 2010 introduces a new regime **8–20** for the conservation of seals which as from January 31, 2011 replaces the Conservation of Seals Act 1970, which is repealed by s.130.The relevant provisions were brought into force in two stages by the Marine (Scotland) Act 2010 (Commencement No.1) Order 2010 (SSI 2010/230) ("the First Commencement Order") with most of the provisions on seal licences coming into force on September 1, 2010 and the remainder of Pt 6 on January 31, 2011.

The Act now provides that killing, injuring or taking a live seal, intentionally or recklessly, is an offence (s.107), with exceptions for interventions to relieve suffering (as detailed in s.108) or in the course of licensed activity (s.109). It is a special offence to harass a seal intentionally or recklessly at a haul-out site, where seals come ashore, e.g. for breeding, as designated by order after consultation with the Natural Environment Research Council (hereafter "NERC") (s.117). A consultation on such haul-out sites was initiated on March 22, 2011 and concluded on June 21.

Licences to kill or take seals may be issued or varied by the Scottish Ministers, on payment of a fee (s.115), and after consultation with the NERC (s.116(1)) (to whose advice on management of seal populations they must have regard—s.125). The purposes for which a licence may be granted are set out in s.110(1) and include scientific, research or educational purposes, conservation of natural habitats or of seals or other wild animals, birds or wild plants and preventing serious damage to fisheries or fish farms, but the consent of Scottish Natural Heritage is also required before a licence is granted under s.110(1)(b)–(e) (for conservation reasons) in protected areas as defined in s.116(2). These protected areas include various marine protected areas as defined in ss.67 et seq. and other special sites such as SSSIs and European sites.

There are various restrictions on the methods of killing or taking seals under a licence (s.111); compulsory conditions, such as the maximum number of seals to be taken, limitations on shooting and the areas in which seals may be taken, are set out in s.112; and a report on the use of the licence must be submitted in terms of s.113. Licences can be varied or revoked at any time (s.114) but the Scottish Ministers must consult the NERC before varying a licence and obtain the consent of Scottish Natural Heritage to variation of a licence relating to a protected area granted for the purposes set out in s.110(1)(b)–(e).

The Scottish Ministers, after consultation with the NERC, may also designate seal conservation areas to ensure the proper conservation of seals (s.118) and the granting of seal licences is then restricted in terms of s.119 to cases in which there is no satisfactory alternative way of achieving the purpose of the licence and the killing or taking will not be detrimental to the maintenance of any species of seal at a favourable conservation status.

Various supplementary powers are granted. The Scottish Ministers, after consultation with the NERC, are empowered to authorise any person to enter land to obtain information about seals (s.120) or to kill or take seals in accordance with a seal licence granted for the purpose of preventing seals from causing serious damage to fisheries or fish farms (s.121), in both cases after notifying the occupier of the land in terms of s.122. The persons authorised must produce evidence of the authorisation if asked (s.123) and it is an offence to prevent them or obstruct them intentionally or recklessly (s.124). Police are given powers of search and seizure where there is reasonable cause of suspicion of commission of an offence (s.126); seals or seal skins or anything possessed or controlled at the time of the offence and capable of being used in connection with it may be forfeited (s.127); and the penalties for the various offences are set out in s.128.

Under s.129 the Scottish Ministers must review and publish a report on the operation of the seal licensing regime (the provisions on seal licences— s.129(4)) within five years of the time when s.110 comes into operation (September 1, 2010) and every five years from publication of a report thereafter and they must have regard to their most recent report in performing their functions under the regime. In carrying out the review they must take account of scientific evidence and other relevant matters and consult with the NERC and other appropriate persons (s.129(2)).

8–31   The Marine and Coastal Access Act 2009 Pt 7 Ch.2 (ss.202–214) and Sch.22 Pt 5(a) makes a number of modifications to the Sea Fisheries (Shellfish) Act 1967. Of these ss.203, 204, 206, 207, 209, 210, 211(1) and (3), 214 and Sch.22 Pt 5(A) are extended to Scotland by the Marine (Scotland) Act 2010 ss.160 and 161, which also make other changes. These changes take effect from February 24, 2011 by virtue of the Second Commencement Order, art.2 (with transitional provisions in art.4).

fn.94. The 1997 Act is repealed by the 2009 Act Sch.22, Pt 5(A).

8–32   **fn.95.** Sch.1 is amended by the 2010 Act s.160(3) to add a new sub-para.6(2) requiring the Minister to have regard to the powers and duties of the Crown Estate Commissioners where the order relates to the sea shore belonging to the Crown and by the 2010 Act s.161(5) to amend para.4(2) to substitute for "The appropriate Minister shall" "The Scottish Ministers may, and in the case of receiving an objection raising a material concern under paragraph 3 above, must". Paragraphs 4(1) and (5) are repealed by the 2009 Act Sch.22, Pt 5(A) in consequence of the modifications made by the 2009 Act s.214, applied to Scotland by the 2010 Act ss.161(1)(g) and (4), with the exception of the modification made by s.214(2)(b) which amends para.4(2) in the sense noted above.

fn.96. The 2010 Act s.160(1) repeals the 1967 Act s.1(4), requiring the consent of the Crown Estate Commissioners to grant of an order affecting the sea shore owned by the Crown and s.160(2) applies to Scotland s.203 of the 2009 Act which replaces s.1(6) of the 1967 Act with a new s.1(6) to 1(14), allowing the variation of an order where a permitted development prevents or renders impracticable the exercise of a several fishery or regulation of a fishery; the 2010 Act s.161(2) adds subs.(14A) replacing the reference to the Town and Country Planning Act 1990 in s.1(14) with the Town and Country Planning (Scotland) Act 1997.

fn.100. The 2009 Act s.204, applied to Scotland by the 2010 Act s.161(1)(a), **8–33** and brought into force with the other provisions mentioned below, by the Second Commencement Order, replaces the references in the 1967 Act s.3 to improving and cultivating a fishery with references to regulating it and adds s.3(2A) allowing recoupment of the costs of obtaining the order from tolls or royalties imposed. Section 207, applied by s.161(1)(c), adds subss.(6) and (7) to provide for enforcement of restrictions and regulations made by grantees as well as those contained in an order itself.

fn.101. Section 209, applied to Scotland by the 2010 Act s.161(1)(d), provides that where licences are granted a register of them must be kept.

The 2009 Act ss.210 and 211(1) and (3), applied to Scotland by the 2010 Act **8–35** ss.161(1)(e) and (f) respectively, amend the 1967 Act s.7 to cover private shellfish beds as well as private oyster beds and add provisions on the use of implements of fishing, while the 2010 Act s.161(3) increases the maximum fine which can be imposed under s.7(4) to £50,000.

fn.105. The provision on sale in market overt in s.7(3) was repealed by the Sale of Goods (Amendment) Act 1994 s.2(2) in consequence of the repeal of the Sale of Goods Act 1979 s.22(1) on sale in market overt generally.

The Import of Live Fish (Scotland) Act 1978 will be repealed by the Wildlife **8–37** and Natural Environment (Scotland) Act 2011 (asp 6) s.25(2) and Sch. Pt 2 in the light of the extensive provisions on control over the introduction of invasive species which will be introduced by that Act—see paras **9–29** and **9–94** below.

fn.217. In *Pullar v Gauldie*, Unreported August 25, 2004, Arbroath Sh. Ct, the **8–76** sheriff held that, apart from the reservation of a servitude right of access which he held had been made, there would have been an implied right of access in order to exercise the relevant salmon fishings in the sea; *Conveyancing 2010*, pp.179–180.

fn.218. *Tummel Valley Leisure Ltd v Sudjic*, 2010 S.L.T. (Sh. Ct) 170—held that the pursuers holding fishing rights should be able to fish by any lawful means and order to remove decking which restricted fishing of whole pool in which they had rights.

8–113 and On the proposed repeal of the Import of Live Fish (Scotland) Act 1978 see
8–145 para.**8–37** above.

8–149 **fn.430.** The Scotland Act 1998, s.111 is amended by the Marine and Coastal
Access Act 2009, s.231 to extend the species covered to lampreys, smelt and
shad and to add a new subs.(6) to allow an order under subs.(1) to vary the
species covered.

8–153 The Town and Country Planning (Prescribed Date) (Scotland) Regulations
2010 (SSI 2010/61) amend the 2007 Regulations (SSI 2007/123) to postpone
to March 31, 2013 the date by which planning permission is required in marine
fish farms using equipment placed or assembled before April 1, 2007, in the
absence of prior grant or refusal of permission. The 2007 Regulations are
further amended by the Town and Country Planning (Marine Fish Farming)
(Scotland) Amendment Regulations 2011 (SSI 2011/145) and now cover
shellfish.

The Marine (Scotland) Act 2010 s.63, brought into force from April 6, 2011
by the Second Commencement Order (SSI 2011/58), amends the Town and
Country Planning (Scotland) Act 1997 s.26(1) by adding to the reference to
s.26AA a reference to a new s.26AB allowing the Scottish Ministers, with
agreement of the relevant planning authority, to make an order that marine
fish farming is not "development" for the purposes of the Act. The Town and
Country Planning (Marine Fish Farms Permitted Development) (Scotland)
Order 2011 (SSI 2011/144) specifies the developments for which no specific
application for planning permission is required.

Part II of the Environmental Impact Assessment (Scotland) Regulations
1999 (SS1 1999/1), as amended, is replaced by the consolidating and updated
Town and Country Planning (Environmental Impact Assessment) (Scotland)
Regulations 2011 (SSI 2011/139).

The Wildlife and Natural Environment (Scotland) Bill 2010 received the Royal **9–29 et**
Assent on April 7, 2011 as the Wildlife and Natural Environment (Scotland) **seq.**
Act 2011 (asp 6) ("the Wildlife Act"). When it is brought fully into force it will
bring protection of game birds and other animals and prevention of poaching
within the Wildlife and Countryside Act 1981 by substantial amendment of
that Act in relation to Scotland; it will do away with game licences; it will
make revised provision on protection of badgers and on muirburn; it will
extend controls over introduction of non-native species by further
amendment of the 1981 Act; it will require triennial reports on compliance
with the biodiversity duty imposed on public bodies under the Nature
Conservation (Scotland) Act 2004 s.2; and it will make amendments to the
SSSI regime. The details are dealt with in the appropriate paragraphs below
and the changes when made will make obsolete much of the present text. The
first steps towards bringing it into force were taken by the Wildlife and Natural
Environment (Scotland) Act 2011 (Commencement No.1) Order (SSI 2011/
279), as amended by the Amendment Order SS1 2011/287 ("the
Commencement Order").

One other major change is that, while new measures are being introduced
which are intended to replace them, the Wildlife Act s.25 and the Sch. Pt 2, will
make a holocaust of the Game Laws and related legislation treated in paras **9–
29 et seq.** and provisions on imported animals and fish. The result will be the
repeal of the Game (Scotland) Act 1772; the Night Poaching Act 1828; the
Game Act 1831, as extended to Scotland by the Game Licenses (*sic*) Act 1860
s.13; the Game (Scotland) Act 1832 [the Day Trespass Act 1832]; the Night
Poaching Act 1844; the Hares (Scotland) Act 1848; the Game Licenses Act
1860; the Poaching Prevention Act 1862; the Game Laws Amendment
(Scotland) Act 1877; the Ground Game Act 1880 s.4 (exemption from
holding a game licence); the Customs and Inland Revenue Act 1883 (game
licences); the Hares Preservation Act 1892; the Finance Act 1924 (game
licences); the Destructive Imported Animals Act 1932; the Finance Act 1937
s.5 and Sch.2 (game licences); the Agriculture (Scotland) Act 1948 s.53
(exemption from holding a game licence); the Local Government (Scotland)
Act 1966 s.44, Sch.4 Pt II—entries on the Game Licenses Act 1860 and
Customs and Inland Revenue Act 1883; the Game Act 1970; the Import of
Live Fish (Scotland) Act 1978; the Deer (Scotland) Act 1996 s.38 (exemption
from holding a game licence); the Protection of Wild Mammals (Scotland) Act
2002 Sch. paras 1 and 2 (which already repeal the Game (Scotland) Act 1832,
s.4 and exceptions 3 and 4 in the Game Licences Act 1860 s.5 so far as referring
to Scotland); and the Marine (Scotland) Act 2010 s.104 (amending the 1981
Act s.16 on the grant of licences under the Act, which is amended by the
Wildlife Act s.18(2) to similar effect). These provisions so far as relating to
game and game licences were brought into force as from June 29, 2011 by the
amended Commencement Order.

In Pt 7, s.41 of the Wildlife Act makes provision for application to the
Crown of the 1981 Act, the Protection of Badgers Act 1992 and the Deer
(Scotland) Act 1996, in general applying them, but in some cases requiring
consent of a relevant authority and relieving the Crown of criminal liability
while allowing an enforcing authority to apply to the Court of Session for a
declaration that an act is unlawful.

9–39   Now that the repeals made by the Wildlife Act have taken effect only the provisions for licensing of dealers in venison in the Deer (Scotland) Act 1996 remain.

9–48   The Wildlife Act s.11(2) will insert s.12YA in the Wildlife and Countryside Act 1981 giving effect to Sch.7; s.11(3) will repeal the 1981 Act, s.12; s.11(4) will give a new title to the 1981 Act, Sch.7 "Amendment of Acts in Relation to Night Shooting of Hares and Rabbits" and substitute s.12YA for s.12 in the section reference.

9–54 and   The Wildlife Act s.25(1) and the Sch. Pt 1, brought into force from June 29,
fn.156.   2011 by the Commencement Order modifies the Agriculture (Scotland) Act 1948 s.39(2) to replace the reference to game within the meaning of the Game (Scotland) Act 1772 with a reference to (a) black grouse, common pheasant, grey partridge, ptarmigan, red grouse or red-legged partridge in the close season for that bird within the meaning of the 1981 Act s.2(4) and (b) brown hare or mountain hare in the close season for those animals within the meaning of the 1981 Act s.10A(2), so that compliance with a notice does not constitute an offence under the 1981 Act s.1 or s.10A(1) as the case may be.

9–57   **fn.167.** The Public Services Reform (Scotland) Act 2010 s.1 and Sch.1 (modification of enactments) transfers the functions of the Scottish Deer Commission to Scottish Natural Heritage ("SNH") as from August 1, 2010—Public Services Reform (Scotland) Act 2010 (Commencement No.1) Order (SSI 2010/221) art.3(2) and Sch.

9–57   The Wildlife Act Pt 3 (ss.26–32) dealing with deer, in s.26(2), in relation to the functions of SNH will amend the Deer (Scotland) Act 1996 ("the 1996 Act") s.1(1)(a) to refer to conservation of deer native to Scotland and add s.1(2)(d) and (e) to add to the matters it is required to consider the interests of public safety and the need to manage the deer population in urban and peri-urban areas. Section 26(3), in relation to the power of SNH to facilitate exercise of its functions, will amend s.3(1) of the 1996 Act to add s.3(1)(c) allowing it to assist any person or organisation in reaching agreements with third parties and s.3(3) requiring a public body or office-holder issued guidance or advice under s.3(1)(a) to have regard to it in exercising any functions to which the guidance or advice relates. Section 26(4) will remove the restriction on the number of members on a panel set up under the 1996 Act s.4, to nine and s.27 will insert into the 1996 Act a new s.5A, in s.5A(1) requiring the SNH to draw up a code of practice for the purpose of providing practical guidance in respect of deer management. This by s.5A(2) may in particular recommend practice for sustainable deer management, make provision about collaboration in deer management, set out examples of circumstances in which the SNH may seek to secure a control agreement or make a control scheme and may make different provision for different cases, in particular for different circumstances, different times of year or different areas. The code must be reviewed from time to time, may be replaced or revised, must be drawn up, replaced or revised after consultation with persons interested and the proposed code or any proposed replacement or revision must be submitted to the Scottish Ministers for approval (s.5A(3)–(6)) and published by them, so far as approved, modified or replaced no later than the day before it comes into effect (s.5A(11)). The Scottish Ministers can approve the relevant code, with or without modification, or reject it and in case of rejection may instruct SNH to submit a new code or devise their own (s.5A(6) and (7)). The first code and any replacement must be laid before and approved by resolution of the Scottish parliament, any revision must also be laid before the parliament at least 40 days before it is to come into effect (disregarding dissolutions or recesses) and parliament may resolve before the revision comes into effect that it shall not come into effect (s.5A(8)–(10)). The SNH must monitor compliance with the code and have regard to it in exercising its functions under the 1996 Act (s.5A(12)). The proposed code, prepared after consultation, was due to be submitted to Ministers on September 2, 2011.

The Muntjac Keeping (Scotland) Regulations 2011 (SSI 2011/63) made under **9–58** the Destructive Imported Animals Act 1932, as applied to all species of Muntjac deer by the Muntjac Keeping (Scotland) Order 2011 (SSI 2011/172), require a licence, under the conditions set out in the Schedule to the Regulations, for the keeping of Muntjac deer.

fnn.174 and 175. In relation to emergency measures the Wildlife Act s.28(4) will repeal the word "serious" in the 1996 Act s.10(1)(a)(i) and add s.10(1)(a)(ia) "causing damage to their own welfare or the welfare of other deer" and the Wildlife Act s.28(5) will repeal the word "serious" in the 1996 Act s.11.

The Wildlife Act s.28(2) will make detailed amendments to the provisions of **9–59** the 1996 Act s.7 on control agreements to the effect that SNH is to act having had regard to the code of practice on deer management introduced by s.27 and can intervene when deer or steps taken or not taken for the purposes of deer management have caused or procured, etc. damage, including now damage to the welfare of deer or public interests of a social, economic or environmental nature. Reference in s.7(1) to reduction in number of deer will then be replaced by a more general provision that measures require to be taken in relation to the management of deer for the remedying of the damage. In s.7(3) reference will again be added to the code of practice; s.7(4) will now begin "After [the SNH] has given notice to such owners and occupiers as it considers to be substantially interested" that it has formed a view that steps need to be taken; s.7(5)(f) will be added reading "set out measures, or steps towards taking such measures, which the owners or occupiers are to take during each twelve month period for which the agreement has effect"; also s.7(7) requiring SNH to review control agreements at least annually for compliance.

The Wildlife Act s.28(3) will make substantial amendments to the 1996 Act s.8 on control schemes. Section 28(3)(a) will add s.8(A1) to provide that where the SNH has given notice under s.7(4) and either (i) it is satisfied that it is not possible to secure a control agreement or that a control agreement is not being carried out or (ii) six months have elapsed with no agreement reached and SNH still thinks that action is required then under a new s.8(1) the SNH, having had regard to the code of practice on deer management, and being satisfied that action is necessary for the purposes mentioned in s.7(1) or 7(3) of the 1996 Act must make a control scheme to carry out the necessary measures; s.28(3)(b) will qualify s.8(2) with an exception where the purpose of the control agreement is to remedy damage caused, directly or indirectly, by deer or steps taken or not taken for the purposes of deer management; s.28(3)(c) will repeal s.8(5) (cf. **fn.178**) which does not allow a requirement in a control scheme to construct a fence; and s.28(3)(d) will add s.8(7A) requiring SNH to review any confirmed control scheme at least annually for compliance.

Section 28(6) will make considerable changes to the procedure for making control schemes set out in the 1996 Act Sch.2, removing reference to a potential local enquiry, requiring publicity in such manner as the SNH or Scottish Ministers respectively think fit, rather than by publication in the *Edinburgh Gazette* and local newspapers, and replacing application to the Court of Session by a person aggrieved by the making of the control scheme by appeal to the Scottish Land Court, the appeal being determined on its merits rather than by review.

9–62 The Wildlife Act s.29(2) will repeal the reference to s.26 in the 1996 Act s.5(6) and replace paras (a) and (b) to read:

> "(a) the taking or killing is necessary (i) to prevent damage to any crops, pasture or human or animal foodstuffs on any agricultural land which forms part of that land or (ii) to prevent damage to any enclosed woodland which forms part of that land or (b) the taking or killing is necessary (i) to prevent damage to any unenclosed woodland which forms part of that land; or (ii) to prevent damage, whether directly or indirectly, to the natural heritage generally; or (iii) in the interests of public safety and no other means of control which might reasonably be adopted in the circumstances would be adequate."

It will also add s.5(8) providing that an authorisation under s.5(6) or 5(7) may be to any degree general or specific (including the land referred to) and may be to a particular person or to a category of persons.

9–63 The Wildlife Act s.29(3) will amend the 1996 Act s.26 to remove the reference to "serious" in the title, to remove the reference to s.5 in s.26(1) and the word "serious", allowing the occupier to act where damage is likely, and to add s.26(1A) removing the right to act during any period fixed by order under s.5(1) in relation to the sex and species of deer concerned.

fn.188. Section 31 will amend the 1996 Act s.25 to insert para.(za) reading "a deer which is starving and which has no reasonable chance of recovering".

9–64 fn.192. The Wildlife Act s.29(4) will amend the 1996 Act s.37(1) to insert an exception set out in a new s.37(1A) which provides that s.37(1) does not apply to an authorisation under s.5(6) to the occupier of land falling within s.26(1)(a) or (b), i.e. arable land etc. or enclosed woodland, or, if authorised by the occupier, the owner of the land, an employee of the owner, or an employee of the occupier or other person normally resident on the land, where the purpose of the authorisation is to prevent damage within s.5(6)(a)—see para.**9–62** above.

9–68 The Wildlife Act s.30, will insert a new heading before the 1996 Act s.17 reading "Unlawful killing, taking and injuring deer", repeal s.17(4) and replace it with new provisions in ss.17A and 17B for a register of persons competent to shoot deer. Under s.17A the register would be set up and operated by the Scottish Ministers under regulations which would prohibit anyone from shooting deer, except for a purpose mentioned in s.25, unless registered or supervised by a registered person and would require registered persons or owners or occupiers of land to submit cull returns, as specified, to SNH. The regulations would make detailed provisions on applications, etc.

and would be made after consultation with interested persons. Section 17B provides that if the power to make regulations is not exercised by April 1, 2014 the SNH must carry out a review of the levels of competence among persons who shoot deer in Scotland and the effect of such levels on deer welfare, with due consultation, and publish a report of it.

The Wildlife Act subss.30(5)–(9) will insert the italic heading "Other offences and attempts to commit offences" before the 1996 Act s.18, make consequential changes on penalties in ss.30, 31and Sch.3 in the light of s.17A (see paras **9–70 fn.205** and **9–72 fnn.214** and **215**) and insert in s.45(1) (interpretation) a definition of "registered person" and "shoot" and "shooting", the latter meaning, as before, discharge and discharging a firearm of a class prescribed in an order under s.21(1).

fn.213. The Wildlife Act s.32(2) will amend the 1996 Act s.29 to make the **9–72** existing text subs.(1) and add s.29(2) reading, "[w]here the affairs of a body corporate are managed by its members, subsection (1) applies in relation to the acts and defaults of a member in connection with his functions of management as if he were a director of the body corporate" and s.32(3) will add a new s.29A to deal with offences by a Scottish partnership or other unincorporated association, making partners or purported partners and persons managing or controlling or purporting to manage or control an association liable along with the partnership or association in case of consent, connivance or neglect in relation to commission of an offence.

The Wildlife Act s.34, brought into force from August 1, 2011 by the **9–75** Commencement Order makes substantial changes to the Hill Farming Act 1946 ("the 1946 Act") ss.23–27 on muirburn. Section 41(2) inserts a new s.27A providing that ss.23–27, including orders made under s.23B, bind the Crown, without imposing criminal liability but allowing application to the Court of Session to declare contraventions unlawful, and under the proviso that the sections apply to persons in the public service of the Crown as they apply to other persons.

The Wildlife Act s.34(2) substitutes a new s.23 in the 1946 Act allowing **9–76** muirburn only in the muirburn season, which is to consist of a standard season from October 1 to April 15 (s.23(3)) or an extended season, from April 16 to 30 (s.23(4)). Muirburn may be made only by the proprietor of the land or a person authorised in writing by him or on his behalf (s.23(5)). Section 34(3) revises s.23A of the 1946 Act, which was added by the Climate Change (Scotland) Act 2009 (asp 12) s.58, to allow variation of the muirburn season in the light of the effects of climate change. Section 23A(1) now allows extension or reduction of the standard or extended muirburn season; s.23A(1A) is added to allow different provision for different purposes, such as land at different altitudes or standard or extended muirburn seasons in different years; in s.23A(2) "in relation to climate change" becomes subs.(a) and subss.(b) and (c) are added to refer to the purposes of conserving, restoring, enhancing or managing the natural environment and the purposes of public safety respectively; in subs.(3) the reference to commencement of the 2009 Act is replaced by reference to the Wildlife Act; s.34(4) adds a new s.23B to the 1946 Act providing for further regulation of making muirburn by order, exercisable by statutory instrument (s.23B(6)–(7)), providing for such matters as notice, making of representations or objections and the imposition of conditions; s.34(4) also adds a new s.23C to the 1946 Act allowing the

Scottish Ministers to grant a licence to make muirburn during any period other than the muirburn season for the purposes of conserving, restoring, enhancing or managing the natural environment, research or public safety (s.23C(4))—the power is delegable to SNH by written direction (s.23C(6)–(10)—and there is power to make further provision by regulations, again exercisable by statutory instrument (s.23C(11)–(13)).

9–77   The Wildlife Act s.34(6) revises s.25 of the 1946 Act to insert a new para.(za) reading:

> "makes muirburn or causes or procures the making of muirburn on any land otherwise than (i) during the muirburn season in accordance with section 23; or (ii) in accordance with a licence granted under section 23C"

and repeals para.(c) in the light of the new provisions on notice in the revised s.26 of the 1946 Act. The Wildlife Act s.34(7) revises s.26 of the 1946 Act by giving it a new title "Notice as to muirburn: general requirement" and substituting for the present provisions in s.26 more detailed requirements (noting that s.23B(1) may make other provision and that s.24(2) makes provision on other notice to be given by a tenant); these requirements in general are that written notice of what is intended must be given to the proprietor of the proposed muirburn site, or any person purporting to be authorised by the proprietor to receive it, and any occupier of land situated within 1 kilometre of the site, after expiry of the previous muirburn season and not less than seven days before starting; the person given notice may ask for further particulars. The Wildlife Act s.34(8) then inserts a new s.26A on the giving of muirburn notices under s.24(2) (tenants) or s.26 which sets out detailed requirements, which include personal delivery, the possibility of electronic communication and affixing notice to some conspicuous object on the land where the occupier cannot be ascertained after reasonable enquiry.

9–78   The Wildlife Act s.34(9) amends the 1946 Act s.24 to add subs.24(2A) providing that notice to the proprietor under s.24(2) must be in writing and may be given to any person purporting to be authorised by the proprietor to receive it.

9–80   The Wildlife Act s.34(9) amends the 1946 Act s.27 to give it a new title "Penalties etc. for offences" and replaces the words "twenty-three or section twenty-five" with "25 or 26(10)" and s.35 adds after the 1946 Act s.34 a new s.34A on offences by bodies corporate, Scottish partnerships etc. under the 1946 Act which mirrors the provisions referred to in para.**9–72** above.

9–81   A. McKie, "Protections with Legs" (2010) 55(1) J.L.S. 48—on European protected species and planning permission.

9–83 and   The Wildlife Act makes substantial amendments to the Wildlife and
9–84   Countryside Act 1981 Act ("the 1981 Act") with a view to bringing game birds further within the protection of the general legislation on protection of birds.

9–83   The Wildlife Act s.3 amends the 1981 Act by revising the italic heading before s.1 to read "Protection of wild birds, their nests and eggs and prevention of poaching", replacing s.1(6) with a provision that "wild bird" defined in s.27(1) does not include any bird bred in captivity unless (a) it has been lawfully released or allowed to escape as part of a re-population or re-introduction programme or (b) is a mallard, grey or red-legged partridge, common pheasant or red grouse no longer in captivity and not in the place where it was reared.

fn.247. The Wildlife Act s.2 repeals in s.27(1) the definition of "game bird" and in the definition of "wild bird" the words "or, except in sections 5 and 16, any game bird".

The Wildlife Act s.3(4) adds to the title of the 1981 Act s.2 ":acts by certain **9–84** persons outside close season"; inserts a new subs.(1A) referring to persons with a legal right or permission to kill or take; inserts in the 1981 Act s.2(3) after "Christmas Day" "in relation to those birds included in Part I of Schedule 2 which are also included in Part IA of that Schedule"; inserts new subss.(3A), (3B) and (3C) allowing limited taking outside the close season; inserts in s.2(4) the close seasons for pheasants (February 2–September 30), partridges (February 2–August 31), black grouse (December 11–August 19 following) and ptarmigan and red grouse (December 11–August 11 following); amends s.2(7) to cover such persons as are considered appropriate; s.3(5) amends the 1981 Act Sch.2 Pt I to add black and red grouse, grey and red-legged partridge, common pheasant and ptarmigan and s.3(6) adds a new Sch.2 Pt IA (birds included in Pt I which may not be killed or taken on Sundays or Christmas Day) with 17 entries from coot to woodcock.

fn.260. Wild Birds (Special Protection in Severe Weather) (Scotland) Order **9–84 and** 2010 (SSI 2010/4), (No.2) Order (SSI 2010/438) and (No.3) Order (SSI 2010/ **9–85** 470)—limited additional protection outside the close season.
  The Wildlife Act s.4 will repeal the 1981 Act s.3 on areas of special protection for wild birds with consequential amendment of ss.4, 16 and 26 so far as referring to s.3.

The Wildlife Act s.4(4A), in the 1981 Act s.5(5), for "game bird" substitutes **9–86** "grouse, mallard, partridge or pheasant included in Part I of Schedule 2".

The Wildlife Act s.5(2) amends the 1981 Act s.2(4) and 2(6) to substitute **9–87** "section 1, this section and section 6" for "this section and section 1"; s.5(3)(a) amends the 1981 Act, s.6(1)(a) by repealing the words "other" to "3" and inserting "other than (i) a bird included in Part I of Schedule 3 (see also subsection (5)), (ii) a bird included in Part IA of that Schedule to which subsection (1A) applies or (iii) an egg to which subsection (1B) applies or any part of such egg"; s.5(3)(b) inserts subss.(1A) and (1B) allowing various exceptions; s.5(3)(c) amends the 1981 Act s.6(2)(a) to insert Pt IIA after Pt II and "see also subsections (5B) and (6)" after "Schedule 3".
  The Wildlife Act s.5(3)(d) substitutes for the 1981 Act s.6(5) a new s.6(5) providing that a reference to a bird included in Sch.3 Pt I is to a bird bred in captivity, ringed or marked in accordance with regulations made by the Scottish Ministers and not lawfully released or allowed to escape as part of a re-population or re-introduction programme and adds s.6(5A) allowing regulations to make different provision for different birds or different provisions of the section; s.5(3)(e) inserts a new s.6(5B) providing that a reference to a bird included in Sch.3 Pt IIA is to a bird killed outside its close season by a person with a legal right or permission to do so; s.5(3)(f) substitutes

a new s.6(6) providing that a reference to a bird included in Sch.3 Pt III is, during the period from September 1 in any year to February 28 in the following year, to a bird included in that Part.

The Wildlife Act s.5(4)(a) inserts in the 1981 Act Sch.3, Pt IA (listing birds alive if taken in captivity or by certain persons outside close season or during first 28 days of close season), namely, red grouse, mallard, grey and red-legged partridge and common pheasant; s.5(4)(b) inserts Pt IIA (listing birds dead if killed outside close season by certain persons) with 17 entries from coot to woodcock (but differing from the list in Sch 2, Pt IA); s.5(4)(c) repeals in the 1981 Act Sch.3, Pt III (listing birds which may be sold dead from September 1 to February 28) 11 entries from coot to woodcock.

fn.277. Wildlife and Countryside Act 1981 (Variation of Schedule 4) (Scotland) Order 2009 (SSI 2009/418) and Wildlife and Countryside Act 1981 (Registration and Ringing of Certain Captive Birds) (Scotland) Regulations (SSI 2009/419) revoke earlier Regulations from 1982–1994.

9–90 The Wildlife Act adds a raft of measures to the 1981 Act to replace the existing law on protection of hares and prevention of poaching of hares and rabbits including extensive new provisions on snares and their use, as noted below. Most of these, but not the provisions on snares, were brought into force from June 29, 2011 by the Commencement Order.

The Wildlife Act s.6(2) adds s.10A to the 1981 Act to provide that anyone who in the relevant close season intentionally or recklessly kills, injures or takes any wild animal included in Sch.5A (which is inserted by s.6(5) and covers the mountain hare and brown hare), while the title to the present Sch.5 (protected animals) is amended by s.6(4) to add "under section 9") is guilty of an offence (s.10A(1)). There is a presumption that the animal is wild unless the contrary is shown (s.10A(8)). The close season for mountain hares is March 1 to July 31 and for brown hares February 1 to September 30 (s.10A(2)) but this is variable by the Scottish Ministers by order (s.10A(3)) and a period of special protection not exceeding 14 days outside the close season may also be declared (s.10A(4)–(6)); the orders may apply to the whole or any part of Scotland specified in the order (s.10A(7)).

Section 6(2) also adds s.10B to the 1981 Act providing for exceptions, such as killing an animal disabled beyond recovery, not by the person in question (s.10B(1)); or taking a disabled animal by right or permission in order to tend and release it (s.10B(2)); or action taken by an authorised person to prevent serious damage to livestock etc. before a licence to do so could be obtained (s.10B(3)–(6)); or action taken under the Agriculture (Scotland) Act 1948 s.39 for control of pests or the Animal Health Act 1981 for control of disease (s.10B(7)).

The Wildlife Act s.7(2) amends the 1981 Act to add "and prevention of poaching" to the italic heading before s.9 (protection of certain wild animals); s.7(3) inserts s.11G in the 1981 Act providing that any person who intentionally or recklessly kills, injures or takes any wild animal included in Sch.6A (added by s.7(4) and listing mountain and brown hares and rabbits) is guilty of an offence (with a presumption that the animal in question is wild—s.11G(2)); it also inserts s.11H providing for exceptions—persons with a legal right or permission, seriously disabled animals, action taken under the Agriculture (Scotland) Act 1948 s.39 or the Animal Health Act 1981.

The Wildlife Act s.8 adds s.11I to the 1981 Act on the sale, possession, etc. of wild hares, rabbits, etc. killed or taken unlawfully which will create offences of having in possession or control, selling, offering or exposing for sale or having in possession or transporting for sale, advertising the buying or selling of a relevant animal, part of an animal or anything derived from it, without reasonable excuse (s.11I(1)–(2)); again there is a presumption that the animal was wild unless the contrary is shown (s.11I(3)).

The Wildlife Act s.9 then amends the 1981 Act s.16(3) and (4)(b) appropriately on licensed activity; the Wildlife Act s.10 adds to the 1981 Act, s.22(1)(b), on variation of schedules, Schs 5A and 6A and a new s.22(2ZA) and allows prescription of a close season for the purposes of s.10A for animals added to Sch.5A; the Wildlife Act s.11(2), not yet in force, will add a new s.12YA introducing Sch.7 amending Acts prohibiting night shooting of hares and rabbits; s.11(3) will repeal the 1981 Act s.12; and s.11(4) will give a new title to Sch.7 "Amendment of Acts in relation to Night Shooting of Hares and Rabbits" with a reference to the new s.12ZA.

The Wildlife Act s.12 amends the 1981 Act s.19A entitling it "Single witness evidence in Scotland in certain proceedings" and lists as relevant certain offences under ss.1(1)(a), 6(1) and 6(2) relating to grouse, pheasant, partridge and ptarmigan and offences under ss.1(1)(c), 10A(1), 11G(1) and 11I(1).

fn.283. The Wildlife Act s.33, brought into force from June 29, 2011 by the Commencement Order, makes a considerable number of amendments to strengthen and extend the scope of the Protection of Badgers Act 1992, including possible delegation of licensing powers of the Scottish Ministers to SNH or local authorities.

fn.286. A. Entwhistle, "Beat the BAT Increase", 2011 Prop. L.B. 110-1.

fnn.286 and **287.** The Wildlife Act s.19, brought into force from June 29, 2011 by the Commencement Order, removes 10 animals from horseshoe bats to harbour porpoises from the 1981 Act Sch.6 (animals which may be killed or taken by certain methods) on the ground that they are covered by the 2007 Habitat Regulations. This leaves only badgers, hedgehogs, shrews and red squirrels.

The Wildlife Act will make extensive new provision on snares and their use, **9–92** including provisions on identification of users, rather than imposing a total ban on their use supported by some MSPs.

The Act s.13(2) will amend the 1981 Act s.11, inserting subs.(1A) in relation to s.11(1)(aa) on snares calculated to cause unnecessary suffering, referring to the need for stops on snares, their attachment and avoiding the risk of suspension or drowning and repealing subss.(3)–(3B) and (3D).

Section 13(3) will add a new s.11A setting out an elaborate scheme for identification numbers for persons setting snares (s.11A(1)), tagging of snares showing identification numbers and, for brown hares, rabbits or foxes, what the snare is for (s.11A(2)); identification numbers would be issued by chief constables on application to persons adequately trained on the use of snares and the circumstances where their use is appropriate for predator control (s.11A(3), (4), (7) and (9)), all in accordance with provisions in an order to be made by the Scottish Ministers (s.11A(8)). Failure to comply would be an offence (s.11A(5) and (6)).

Section 13(3) will also add s.11B imposing a duty to inspect snares set at least once every day at intervals of not more than 24 hours to see whether any animal is caught and whether the snare is free-running (as defined more closely in s.11B(4)), releasing or removing any such animal and removing or making free-running any snare which is not free-running (s.11B(2)); s.11C making it an offence, without reasonable excuse, to be in possession of or set a snare on land without the authorisation of the owner or occupier; s.11D setting up a presumption that the identification number on a tag is the identification number of the person who set the snare; s.11E laying down the records to be kept by any person who has an identification number, in particular the location of every snare set; and s.11F imposing an obligation on the Scottish Ministers to carry out reviews of the operation and effect of ss.11 to 11E and orders made thereunder no later than December 31, 2016 and every five years thereafter, laying a report of the reviews before the Scottish Parliament. Under the Act s.13(4) and (5) appropriate amendments would be made to the 1981 Act, s.16(3) on licences to include s.11C and to the 1981 Act s.17 on false statements to add references to identification numbers.

fn.295. Snares (Scotland) Order 2010 (SSI 2010/8) made under the 1981 Act, s.11(3E) and (4A).

9–94 The Wildlife Act will introduce a whole new regime for the control of the introduction of non-native species of animals and plants expanding and adding greatly to the provisions of the 1981 Act ss.14, 14A and 14B.

The Act s.14(2) will substitute the 1981 Act s.14(1) with a new s.14(1) which makes it an offence in general (a) to release or allow to escape from captivity any animal to a place outwith its native range or any animal of a type specified by the Scottish Ministers by order or (b) otherwise to cause any animal outwith control to be at a place outwith its native range (defined more closely in a new s.14P(2) and (3)). A new s.14P(7) will define an animal as including its ova, semen or milt. The Act s.14(2) will also substitute s.14(2) with a new s.14(2) which will make it an offence for any person to plant or otherwise cause to grow any plant in the wild outwith its native range (defined also in s.14P(2) and (3)) and will add to these provisions s.14(2A)–(2C) including a provisions exempting release of the common pheasant and red-legged partridge for shooting (s.14(2A)), but allowing disapplication by order of the Scottish Ministers (s.14(C) and specifying the content of any order (s.14(2B) and (2)(D)). A new s.14P(8) will define a "plant" to include fungi, bulbs, corms and rhizomes and, despite s.27(ZA), seeds and spores. In the 1981 Act s.14(3) "prove" will become "show" and subss.(5) and (6) will be repealed.

The Wildlife Act s.14(3) will insert s.14(ZC) in the 1981 Act with s.14ZC(1) and (2) prohibiting keeping or having in possession or control any invasive animal or plant specified by order of the Scottish Ministers, with a defence of due diligence (s.14ZC(3) and (4)) and compensation for those already having them when control is introduced (s.14ZC(5)). A new s.14P(4) will define "invasive" as one having a significant adverse effect on biodiversity, other environmental interests or social or economic interests.

The Wildlife Act s.14(4) will amend the title of the 1981 Act s.14A to refer to invasive animals and plants and s.14A(1) to apply to any type of animal or plant specified by order of the Scottish Ministers, which by a new s.14A(3) may make different provision for different cases.

The Wildlife Act s.15 will insert a new 1981 Act s.14C providing for a code of practice to be published by the Scottish Ministers, giving practical guidance on the application of ss.14, 14ZC, 14A and 14B, orders made thereunder, species control agreements, species control orders and licences under s.16(4)(c). The requirements of the proposed code are very detailed and wide-ranging and the code is to be laid before and approved by resolution of the Scottish Parliament (as well as any revision or revocation) (as for the code of practice on deer management—see para.**9–57** above). A consultation on a draft code of practice on non-native and invasive non-native species was initiated on March 17, 2011 and ended on June 9, 2011.

The Wildlife Act s.16 will add 13 new sections to the 1981 Act—ss.14D–14P (the interpretation section) dealing with species control orders. Species control orders (s.14D(1)) can be made by a relevant body (the Scottish Ministers, SNH, SEPA or the Forestry Commissioners—s.14P(6)) in respect of premises (which do not include dwellings—s.14P(5)) where there are invasive animals or plants and it has not been possible to secure agreement with the owner or occupier on control or eradication (s.14D(2)) or that person has failed to comply with an agreement (s.14D(3)) or it has not been possible to identify the owner or occupier (s.14D(4)–(6)). Control orders can also be made in emergency without the usual procedure (s.14E)). Section 14F sets out the content of an order; s.14G the written notice normally required; s.14H deals with appeals to the sheriff, who decides on the merits and not by way of review; s.14I sets the time at which the order takes effect; s.14J allows review by the relevant body; s.14K sets out the offences of not carrying out an order or obstructing its operation, without reasonable excuse; s.14L allows the relevant body to act if the order or operations required by it are not carried out, recovering its expenses; ss.14M–14O deal with powers of entry—the normal powers, additional powers exercisable by warrant of the sheriff or a JP, e.g. allowing opening lockfast places, and supplementary provisions, e.g. allowing the person entering to be accompanied and to bring machinery or equipment, leaving the premises secure after entry has been made.

The Wildlife Act s.17 will make a number of consequential changes to the 1981 Act ss.16, 22(1), 24 and 26. Notably the 1981 Act Sch.9 will be repealed.

The Wildlife Act s.18, brought into force from June 29, 2011 by the **9–95** Commencement Order, amends the 1981 Act s.16 on licences, in s.16(3) adding para.(i) to include any social, economic or environmental purpose, qualified by a new s.16(3A), repealing subss.16(8B) and (13), and substituting new subss.(9)–(9ZB) for the present subss.(9)–(9ZC), allowing for delegation by the Scottish Ministers of their powers, provided for by a new s.16A which allows the Scottish Ministers to delegate the granting of licences to SNH or, in specific cases, relating to development of land or demolition of buildings, a local authority, and in general requiring the Scottish Ministers to consult SNH before granting or modifying a licence under s.16(1)–(5). There will be consequential changes to s.26 on regulations, etc. and s.26 will also be amended by the Wildlife Act s.4(4B) referring to orders removing from the 1981 Act Sch.2, Pt I, black grouse, common pheasant, grey partridge, ptarmigan, red grouse or red-legged partridge. The Wildlife Act s.22 will amend various provisions of the 1981 Act on wildlife inspectors and their powers consequential on its provisions, repealing s.6(9) and (10), s.7(6) and (7), amending s.19ZC(3), (5) and (9) and s.19ZD(3), (4) and (10) and repealing s.24(4)(c).

The Wildlife Act also makes substantial changes to the provisions on offences and criminal liability in the 1981 Act. Section 20 will add s.26B to the 1981 Act requiring an annual report on wildlife crime by the Scottish Ministers to the Scottish parliament; s.21 will add s.6(2A), s.7(5A) and s.15(2A) creating the offence of knowingly causing or permitting acts done in contravention of the sections; s.23 will add s.69A to allow, in the case of offences committed by

Scottish partnerships or other unincorporated associations, prosecution of individuals as well as the partnership or association where it is proved that a partner or purported partner or a person concerned in management or control of an association or purporting to act as such consented to or connived at commission of the offence or commission of the offence was attributable to his neglect; s.24 will add s.18A to impose vicarious liability in relation to relevant offences as defined in s.18A(6) committed by an employee or agent and s.18B to impose vicarious liability where such an offence is committed by someone providing relevant services as defined in s.18B(5) and (6); in both cases ignorance is a defence if it is shown that the employer, etc. took all reasonable steps and exercised all due diligence to prevent commission of the offence.

9–97   Under the Public Services Reform (Scotland) Act 2010 s.2, SNH takes over the functions of the Advisory Committee on SSSIs.

fn.319. The Wildlife Act s.38, brought into force from June 29, 2011 along with ss.37, 39 and 40 by the Commencement Order, amends the Nature Conservation (Scotland) Act ("the 2004 Act") s.9 on denotification to insert new subss.(5) and (6) on damage caused by operations permitted by a public body or office holder which results in SNH deciding on revocation or modification of an SSSI notification.

fn.320. The Wildlife Act s.37(2) adds s.5A to the 2004 Act to allow for the combination of two or more SSSIs by notification where SNH considers that they should be combined (s.5A(1)). The 2004 Act, s.3(4)–(7) is adapted (s.5A(2)–(3)); s.5A(4) will require SNH to give appropriate public notice of its notification (s.5A(4)) and the combination will not allow the addition of land not already included in at least one site or the addition of operations requiring consent, other than by their extension to land in the combined site (s.5A(5)); in the 2004 Act, s.48(11)(a) (notices etc) "5A(1)" is inserted after "5(1)" and the definitions of SSSI and SSSI notification in s.58(1) are appropriately adapted.

fn.330. The Wildlife Act s.39(4) amends the 2004 Act s.17(1) to add para.(ca) "in accordance with a control scheme made under section 8 of the Deer (Scotland) Act 1996" and para.(f) "if that operation is of a type described by order made by the Scottish Ministers" and s.17(4) to substitute "operation in respect of which section 13 applies" for the words from "owner" to "functions".

fn.335. The Wildlife Act s.39(2) amends the 2004 Act s.13(1) to include operations caused or permitted to be carried out on land owned or occupied by the public body or office-holder.

fn.336. The Wildlife Act s.39(3)(a) amends the 2004 Act s.14(1) to add paras (ca) and (f) in the same terms as in s.17(1)—see **fn.330** above; s.39(3)(b) adds to s.14(2) "or cause or permit to be carried out"; s.39(3)(c) substitutes in s.14(3)(a)(i) "is proposed that the operation be commenced" for "proposes etc.", in s.14(3)(b) adds after "way" "or causes or permits the operation to be carried out only in such a way" and in s.14(3)(c) after "operation" "or, as the case may be, in causing or permitting the carrying out of the operation"; s.39(3)(d) substitutes in s.14(4)(a) for [carries out] "an operation for" [carries out] "or causes or permits the carrying out of an operation in circumstances in" [which it would ... require consent].

fn.337. The Wildlife Act s.40 inserts, as a further means of civil enforcement, after the 2004 Act s.20, a new s.20A with elaborate provisions for restoration notices issued by SNH (s.20A(2)–(7)) where a responsible person has committed an offence under s.19(1) or an offence under s.19(3) in respect of an operation which has damaged a natural feature specified in an SSSI notification (s.20A(1)). If the responsible person gives notice of intention to comply within 28 days that discharges him from liability to conviction for the offence (s.20A(10)) but failure to comply with the requirements of the restoration notice without reasonable excuse is an offence (s.20A(11)) and SNH may carry out the operations required and recover expenses reasonably incurred (s.20A(12)). Where the restoration notice has been wrongly given it may be withdrawn with compensation (s.20A(8)–(9)). There are consequential amendments to ss.14(1), 17(1), 44(1) (powers of entry) and Sch.4, para.1(1)(b) of the 2004 Act and to the Rehabilitation of Offenders Act 1974 s.8B(1) and the Criminal Procedure (Scotland) 1995 ss.69(7), 101 and 166.

(e) Marine nature reserves. The provisions of the Wildlife and Countryside **9–101** Act 1981 ss.36 and 37 and Sch.12 on the creation of marine nature reserves are repealed by the Marine (Scotland) Act 2010 Sch.4, Pt 2 para.5 as they are superseded by the wider provisions of the 2010 Act on marine protection and enhancement in the Scottish marine area.

The Marine Bills referred to became respectively the Marine (Scotland) Act 2010 (asp 5) ("the 2010 Act") and the Marine and Coastal Access Act 2009 ("the 2009 Act") and many of the provisions of the latter are applied to Scotland by reason of amendment of UK provisions or as specifically detailed in s.323(2)–(4). The two Acts mesh together to provide comprehensive measures on the protection of the marine environment. The scheme of the legislation is to combine UK and Scottish measures, with the 2009 Act dealing with the Scottish area of the sea which lies beyond the limits of the territorial sea adjacent to the United Kingdom but which falls within the areas over which the United Kingdom claims jurisdiction, as explained below (2009 Act ss.41 and 42) and the 2010 Act dealing with the Scottish marine area, which covers the area of sea within the seaward limits of the territorial sea adjacent to Scotland (including the bed and subsoil of the sea) (2010 Act s.1).

The "sea" in general is the area submerged at mean high water spring tide and the waters of every estuary, river or channel so far as the tide flows at mean high water spring tide (2009 Act s.42; 2010 Act s.2) but for the purpose of Pt 5 of the 2010 Act on marine protection and enhancement the "sea" excludes waters upstream of the fresh-water limit of estuarial waters (s.66). "Estuarial waters" in turn are defined as waters within the limits of transitional waters within the meaning of Directive 2000/60/EC establishing a framework for Community action on water policy, as amended from time to time (s.65(2)).

The provisions of the two Acts are too complex and extensive for detailed treatment in this work—the 2009 Act consists of 325 sections and 22 Schedules and the 2010 Act of 168 sections and 5 Schedules—but the main thrust of the legislation is to create a UK-wide Marine Management Organisation ("the MMO") (2009 Act ss.1–3 and Schs 1 and 2) with the general objective of contributing to sustainable development in carrying out its various functions, some of which, particularly on fisheries, are transferred to it by Pt 1 Ch.2 of the

Act, and to provide for various protected areas within the limits over which jurisdiction is claimed. There are three relevant limits in relation to protected areas, (a) the territorial sea adjacent to the United Kingdom, (b) the exclusive economic zone beyond the territorial sea to be designated by Order in Council under s.41(2), and (c) the UK area of the continental shelf so far as that extends beyond any designated exclusive economic zone (2009 Act s.42(1))

The 2009 Act s.49 distinguishes various planning regions of which two are the Scottish inshore region and the Scottish offshore region, defined respectively in ss.49(1)(c) and 49(1)(d) and s.322. The former comprises the territorial sea adjacent to Scotland, and within it the 2010 Act applies while the 2009 Act does not and the powers granted are exercised by the Scottish Ministers. Beyond that the 2009 Act applies. However, within the Scottish offshore region the powers granted under the 2009 Act are again in general exercised by the Scottish Ministers but there are exceptions mainly because of the reserved powers under the devolution settlement.

The two Acts have common features. The first step in marine planning (2009 Act Pt 3) is the production of a marine policy statement ("MPS") in terms of the 2009 Act Pt 3 Ch.1 (ss.44–48 and Sch.5). The second step (Pt 3 Ch.2) is the preparation of marine plans, for which purpose the UK marine area is divided into planning regions, defined in s.322, which include the Scottish inshore region and the Scottish offshore region as mentioned above. Each region has a planning authority. For the Scottish inshore region the planning authority is the Scottish Ministers and that region is dealt with by the 2010 Act which sets up a scheme of national and regional marine plans (Pt 3 (ss.5–19 and Sch.1), including limited powers of delegation under ss.12–14). For the Scottish offshore region the planning authority is again the Scottish Ministers (2009 Act s.50(2)(c)) who, like the planning authorities of the other regions, are empowered to prepare a marine plan in terms of ss.51–54 and Sch.6, taking account of the relevant MPS and with limited powers of delegation under ss.55–57. A *Pre-Consultation Draft: Scotland's Marine Plan* was published by the Scottish Government in March 2011 with a view to consultation and finalisation of the Plan in 2012. The marine planning authority must monitor and report on implementation of its plan (s.61; 2010 Act s.16) and there is a limited power to question the validity of an MPS and plans by application to the Court of Session in the case of the Scottish offshore region (ss.62–63), with comparable provision in the 2010 Act ss.17–18 in regard to the Scottish inshore region.

The following Pt 4 of the 2009 Act, paralleled by Pt 4 of the 2010 Act, which was brought into force as from April 6, 2011 by the Second Commencement Order (SSI 2011/58), deals with marine licensing, requiring a marine licence for any licensable marine activity not exempted under ss.74–77 of the 2009 Act or ss.32–34 of the 2010 Act or specially dealt with by ss.78–84 or ss.35–37 respectively, e.g. electricity works and submarine cables. The Marine Licensing (Exempted Activities) (Scottish Offshore Region) Order 2011 (SSI 2011/57), made under s.74 of the 2009 Act, and the Marine Licensing (Exempted Activities) (Scottish Inshore Region) Order 2011 (SSI 2011/204), made under s.32 of the 2010 Act, set out considerable lists of such exempted activities and the conditions under which they are exempt. A consultation on variation of this Order has been opened. The licensable marine activities are in turn defined in ss.61 and 21 respectively and include depositing substances and objects, scuttling vessels, dredging and constructing, altering or improving works in or over the sea or on or under the sea-bed. Licensing follows the usual procedures of application, grant conditionally or unconditionally or refusal, variation, suspension, revocation and appeal (2009 Act ss.67–73; 2010 Act ss.25–31 and 38 and the Marine Licensing Appeals (Scotland) Regulations 2011 (SSI 2011/203)), with, in the case of the 2010 Act ss.22–24, special provision for regulations on prescribed activities which requires notice of the intention to apply, pre-application consultation and a report on compliance with the procedures. The Marine Licensing (Consultees) (Scotland) Order 2011 (SSI 2011/79) provides that in relation to any application under s.25 of the 2010 Act the Commissioners of Northern Lighthouses, the Marine and Coastguard Agency, SEPA and SNH must be consulted.

A register of licences must be kept (2009 Act s.101; 2010 Act s.54) and these provisions are fleshed out by the Marine Licensing (Register of Licensing Information) (Scotland) Regulations 2011 (SSI 2011/80) which inter alia require by reg.3 that there be a single register of applications under ss.101 of the 2009 Act and 54 of the 2010 Act. Fees are prescribed by the Marine Licensing (Fees) (Scotland) Regulations 2011 (SSI 2011/78) in relation to ss.67 of the 2009 Act and 25 of the 2010 Act.

There are powers of delegation (2009 Act ss.98–100; 2010 Act ss.51–53). The requirements on licensing are enforced by the creation of offences, compliance and remediation notices, civil sanctions, stop notices, emergency safety notices and power to take remedial action (2009 Act ss.85–97, 102–110; 2010 Act ss.39–50; 55–62 and relevant Schedules).

Part 5 of the 2009 Act deals with nature conservation and provides in Ch.1 (ss.116–128) for the designation of marine conservation zones (MCZs) in the Scottish offshore region inter alia, with the intention of creating a network of conservation sites consisting of MCZs and other conservation sites (s.123). The 2010 Act makes more elaborate provision in the Scottish marine protection area, namely, the Scottish marine area excluding any waters upstream of the fresh-water limits of estuarial waters (s.65). Under Pt 5 of the Act, brought into force from July 1, 2010 by the First Commencement Order, the Scottish Ministers by designation orders (which may be amended or revoked—s.74) may designate (1) marine protected areas (MPAs) (s.67); (2) Nature Conservation MPAs (ss.68–70), with a duty to designate them to create a network of conservation sites in terms of s.79, paralleling the provisions of the 2009 Act, s.123; (3) Demonstration and Research MPAs (ss.71–72); and (4) Historic MPAs (s.73). Designation orders require publicity and consultation before they are made and publicity after making them (ss.75, 76 and 78), except in case of urgency (s.77). There is provision for advice and guidance by SNH (s.80) and the Scottish Ministers (s.81) and public authorities must have regard to MPAs in exercising their functions (ss.82–84).

To further conservation the Scottish Ministers may make marine conservation orders (ss.85–91), with a delegable power to issue permits authorising acts which would otherwise be unlawful (ss.92–93) and the provisions on conservation are made enforceable by creating offences (ss.94–96), with exceptions in s.97 and a defence that a prohibited act was done in emergency (s.98) and there is also provision for marine management schemes (ss.99–102) and reports to the Scottish Parliament on MPAs (s.103).

Part 8 of the 2009 Act and Pt 7 of the 2010 Act, the latter brought into force mainly as from July 1, 2010 by the First Commencement Order art.2 and completely as from April 6, 2011 by the Second Commencement Order art.2, provide for the appointment of marine enforcement officers who have what are described as common enforcement powers and also specific powers for particular purposes, which are all additional to any powers they may have otherwise. These powers are conferred for the purposes of enforcement of the marine licensing regime, specified marine protection and nature conservation legislation (2009 Act s.237; 2010 Act s.132) and specified fisheries legislation (2009 Act s.238). The common enforcement powers include power to board and inspect vessels and marine installations and to enter and inspect vehicles, to enter and inspect premises, but dwellings only with a warrant, and powers of search, examination and seizure and power to use reasonable force (2009 Act s.246 et seq.; 2010 Act s.133 et seq. and relevant Schedules).

The Marine (Scotland) Act 2010 (Transitional and Consequential Provisions) Order 2011 (SSI 2011/202) makes various transitional arrangements and amendments.

9–102 The National Scenic Areas (Consequential Modifications) (Scotland) Order 2010 (SSI 2010/260) in arts 2–13 makes modifications of various pieces of legislation, primary and secondary, so that references to national scenic areas refer to those designated by direction of the Scottish Ministers under the Planning (Scotland) Act 2006 s.263A.

9–104 In September 2009, 31 new Special Protection Areas for sea-birds were created, extending existing areas out to sea to protect the feeding grounds of guillemots, puffins and gannets.

fn.366 and 9–105. A. McKie, "Tread Warily: Habitats" (2011) 56(1) J.L.S. 48 comments on SNH Guidance, *Habitat Regulations Appraisal of Plans— Guidance for Plan-Making Bodies in Scotland* on appropriate assessment of land-use plans affecting European sites and RAMSAR sites in terms of the 1994 Habitats Regulations, as amended.

R. MacLeod, "Added Capacity" (2010) 55(10) J.L.S. 26—a review of sheriff **11–17 et** court cases on adults with incapacity. **seq.**

fn.62. H. Patrick and N. Smith, *Adult Protection and the Law in Scotland* (2009); A.D. Ward, "Adults with Incapacity: Freedom and Liberty, Rights and Status. (Pt 1) and (Pt 2)", 2011 S.L.T. (News) 21 and 27.

fn.62. In its Annual Report for 2010 (Scot Law Com No.223) the SLC states that in 2011 it will be considering aspects of the law relating to adults with incapacity relating to art.5 of the ECHR.

fn.65. *City of Edinburgh Council v D*, 2011 S.L.T. (Sh. Ct) 15. **11–18**

On the duties of a solicitor in relation to grant or revocation of a continuing **11–19** power of attorney see *Public Guardian, Applicant*, 2011 S.L.T. (Sh. Ct) 66.

fn.90. On remuneration of guardians see *G's Guardian, Applicant*, 2010 S.L.T. **11–22** (Sh. Ct) 35.

Smyth v Rafferty [2011] CSIH 27; 2011 G.W.D. 13-290—lack of capacity and **11–26 and** facility and circumvention pleaded, proof before answer on the latter. **11–27**

fn.169. On *Park, Petitioners* [2008] CSOH 121; 2008 S.L.T. 1026 see J. **11–39** Macleod, "Chalk Dust in the Law of Inhibition" (2009) 13 Edin. L.R. 294.

12–01 **fn.1.** G.L. Gretton and K.G.C. Reid, *Conveyancing*, 4th edn (2011). On the work of the Property Standardisation Group (website *http:// www.psglegal.co.uk* [accessed August 23, 2011]) see I. Macniven, "Now We are 10" (2011) 56(6) J.L.S. 58.

12–03 The problems for purchasers are illustrated by a case reported in *The Herald*, April 9, 2010 where a seller had declared herself insolvent by signing a trust deed for creditors after receiving the purchase price but before the buyer's title was registered; the delay in registration was caused by waiting for an SDLT certificate to allow the registration to proceed.

fn.5. In *Marquess of Linlithgow v Revenue and Customs Commissioners* [2010] CSIH 19; 2010 S.C. 391, discussed in *Conveyancing 2010*, pp.32–33 it was held that in relation to inheritance tax a gift was made on delivery of a disposition of heritable property and not only on registration despite *Burnett's Trs*.

fn.6. G. Junor, "'Offside'—Heritable Obligations and Good Faith", 2009 Prop. L.B. 99-3; J. Macleod, "Offside Goals and Induced Breaches of Contract" (2009) 13 Edin. L.R. 278; P. Webster, "Options for the Offside Goals Rule" (2009) 13 Edin. L.R. 524. See also the SLC *Report on Land Registration* (Scot Law Com No.222, February 2010) paras 14.61–14.65.

12–04 The meaning of a "deed" in Scots law was considered in *Low & Bonar plc v Mercer Ltd* [2010] CSOH 47; 2010 G.W.D. 16-321.

fn.13. *Gibson v Gibson*, 2010 G.W.D. 30-614, Sh. Ct—alleged obligation to repay a sum in case of re-sale of heritable property unenforceable because not in writing, discussed in *Conveyancing 2010*, pp.4–5 and 30.

12–11 **fn.35.** K. Ross, "There may be Trouble Ahead" (2008) 53(1) J.L.S. 48 anticipates the problems which were realised in *PMP Plus* and in the light of which the Keeper has changed his practice—"Uncertain Rights" (2009) 54(8) J.L.S. 17; *Conveyancing 2008*, p.133 et seq.; *Conveyancing 2009*, p.122 et seq.
The SLC *Report on Land Registration* (Scot Law Com. No.222, February, 2010) Pt 6 makes proposals to deal with the issue by amendment of the law to allow creation of "shared plot title sheets" for common areas with provisional shared plot title sheets for common areas in the course of development. There are considerable difficulties with the proposals and it is not clear that they will be enacted.
ARTL was officially launched in December 2009 and an improved version of Registers Direct has also been launched—(2009) 54(9) J.L.S. 15; (2009) 54(10) J.L.S. 15; (2009) 54(12) J.L.S.15; P. Nicholson, "One Giant Leap" (2010) 55(1) J.L.S. 24.
C. Maclean, "ARTL: Friend or Foe?" (2009) 54(10) J.L.S. 42 discusses risk management issues related to the use of ARTL, the use of which continues to expand. Its use, where it is applicable, by members of its panel of solicitors is made compulsory by the Lloyds Banking Group as from September 1, 2010—"Essential ARTL" (2010) 55(6) J.L.S. 32. For critical comment by a solicitor and defences by the Law Society of Scotland's Conveyancing Committee and Registers of Scotland see (2010) 55(7) J.L.S. 8–9; see also D. Preston, "We've

Aye Done It This Way—Not Now" (2010) 55(10) J.L.S. 9; G. Gibson, "Getting to Know You" (2010) 55(10) J.L.S. 56–57 and letters critical of the technology in (2010) J.L.S. 55(9) 10, 55(11) 10, 55(12) 8. See also "Home Reports and ARTL—Members' Letters" in (2010) 78 S.L.G. 74. There are further contributions in "ARTL: Making it Work" (2011) 56(2) J.L.S.10–11 and a report made by P. Nicholson on a "knowledge exchange event" focusing on e-conveyancing and ARTL hosted by Glasgow Caledonian University and Glasgow Solicitors Property Centre "ARTL, by Degrees" (2011) J.L.S. 56(3) 54 and R. Street, "ARTL—Is there a Fix?" (2011) 56(9) J.L.S. 32. The Law Society of Scotland's Conveyancing Committee and Technology Sub-Committee have set up a project group to examine issues relating to the practical problems.

The fees charged by Registers of Scotland were reviewed and were increased in many cases by the Fees in the Registers of Scotland Amendment Order 2010 (SSI 2010/404) but still offer an advantage to those using ARTL; (2010) J.L.S. 55(12) 17.

On the common law liability of the Keeper to pay compensation in respect of **12–13** omission of an alleged right of pre-emption see *Braes v Keeper of the Registers of Scotland* [2009] CSOH 176; 2010 S.L.T. 689; G. Junor, "Pre-emptions, Promises and Prospective Liabilities", 2010 S.L.T. (News) 95; K. Swinton, "Can Braes Bank on the Keeper's Promise?" (2010) 78 S.L.G. 15; *Conveyancing 2009*, pp.128–130.

The SLC *Report on Land Registration* cited above at para.**12–03**, Pt 27 discusses the Keeper's liability for errors more generally.

fn.47 and 12–18 and fn.62. On the question whether an owner is in possession and the date at which that issue is to be decided see *Burr v Keeper of the Registers of Scotland*, Unreported November 12, 2010, Lands Tr., holding that the owner in that case was not in possession and that the date for the decision is either the date at which application is made for rectification of the Register or the date at which the application is disposed of by the Keeper; discussed in *Conveyancing 2010*, pp.160–162.

The Scottish Law Commission's massive *Report on Land Registration*, cited **12–14** above at para.**12–03**, was published in February 2010. Its major recommendation is that the present positive system of land registration created by the 1979 Act, which gives the Keeper his "Midas touch" should be replaced by a system in which the Land Register of Scotland in principle records rather creates rights. This would keep the law of property and the law of land registration more in step. There are, however, many other proposals for change summarised on pp.xxxiii and xxxiv and in the overview in Pt 3 of the Report, setting out the more important points. These points are discussed more fully in the article by G. Gretton, who took over from K. Reid as the lead Commissioner in the project, "The Shape of Things to Come" (2010) 55(3) J.L.S. 22 and in *Conveyancing 2010*, pp.76–79. Some of them are noted elsewhere in this Supplement. Legislation to give effect to the Report is included in the Scottish Government's legislative programme for 2011–2012.

Relevant also are P. O'Connor, "Deferred and Immediate Indefeasibility: Bijural Ambiguity in Registered Land System Titles" (2009) 13 Edin. L.R. 194 and A. Vennard, "Land Registration in the Next 30 Years?" 2010 S.L.T. (News) 1.

fn.51. See also K. Swinton, "The Alice Effect: The Land Register is Always Right or is It?" (2011) 79 S.L.G. 21, commenting on *Willemse v French* [2011] CSOH 51; 2011 G.W.D. 12-282.

12–16 Under the SLC proposals prescription would play a larger role in respect of registered land as registration would not give title immediately to the person registering his right to the land as it generally does at present.

12–18 **fn.67.** The issue whether the holder of a servitude is a proprietor in possession against whom rectification is not possible arose on the facts of *Orkney Housing Association v Atkinson*, Unreported October 15, 2010, Kirkwall Sh. Ct although the point does not seem to have been taken as pointed out in *Conveyancing 2010*, pp.13–14.

12–25 The theory that positive prescription is retrospective in effect was disapproved in *Hamilton v Dumfries and Galloway Council* [2007] CSOH 96 at [33].

12–34 **fn.107.** In *Compugraphics International Ltd v Nicolic* [2011] CSIH 34; 2011 G.W.D. 17-414; 2011 S.C.L.R. 481 it was held on appeal that the title in question was a bounding title not susceptible of interpretation so that the pipework in question was a heritable fixture not a separate tenement and formed an encroachment on the neighbouring land leaving the issue of its retention as depending on possible servitude rights—see para.**22–24**.

12–39 The SLC *Report on Land Registration*, Pt 16, makes new proposals on registration of *a non domino* dispositions, designed to allow acquisition of a prescriptive title to apparently ownerless land where it appears that the owner, if any, has been out of possession for at least seven years and the new claimant or his author has been in possession for at least a year (these periods being variable by subordinate legislation). The initial registration would be shown as provisional.

12–54 The meaning of "an obligation relating to land" has been discussed in several cases; it is not restricted to a real right in land but land must be the main object of the obligation—*Smith v Stuart* [2010] CSIH 29; 2010 S.C. 490 referring to *Barratt (Scotland) Ltd v Keith*, 1993 S.C. 142 and Johnston, *Prescription*, para.6.60; discussed in *Conveyancing 2010*, pp.182–184.

12–56 **fn.187.** On rectification of deeds see D.B. Reid, "Rectification of Deeds: Part 1", 2009 Prop. L.B.103-1; "Rectification of Deeds: Part 2", 2010 Prop. L.B. 104-1.

12–57 On the expressions "use all reasonable endeavours", "use best endeavours" and the like used, e.g. when a party is required to apply for planning permission or obtain some other permission in the context of missives see cases such as *R & D Construction Group Ltd v Hallam Land Management Ltd* [2010] CSIH 96; 2011 S.L.T. 326; 2011 S.C. 286; *Mactaggart & Mickel Homes Ltd v Hunter* [2010] CSOH 130; 2010 G.W.D. 33-683; *Scottish Coal Co Ltd v Danish Forestry Co Ltd* [2010] CSIH 56; 2010 S.C. 729 and para.**18–02** below in the context of leases; G. Junor "'Agreement to Agree'— With All Reasonable Endeavours", 2010 Prop. L.B. 102-4; *Conveyancing 2010*, pp.104–112; R. Wishart and A. Todd, "The 11th Hour; Drafting Agreements to Agree", 2011 Prop. L.B. 112-3.

fn.190. It was held in *Park, Petitioners* [2009] CSOH122; 2009 S.L.T. 871 that missives could not be concluded by fax alone leading to critical comment by J. Ley, "Law out of Step" (2009) 54(10) J.L.S. 56 and to the suggestion by E. Sinclair, "Never Waste a Good Crisis" (2009) 54(11) J.L.S. 56 that electronic missives be introduced more extensively using the Electronic Commerce Act 2000 and related measures, as in ARTL. The SLC *Report on Land Registration*, Pt 34, proposes that the principle of the measures introduced to facilitate ARTL be extended to allow electronic conveyancing generally, at the option of parties; see also S. Brymer, 2009 Prop. L.B. 102-1 at 3; K. Swinton, "Faxed Missives—A Walk in the Park" (2009) S.L.G. 93; E. Sinclair, "E-missives: It's Time for Delivery" (2009) 77 S.L.G. 114; A. Duncan, "Concluding Missives in 2009? On Your Bike" 2009 Prop. L.B.103-5; *Conveyancing 2009*, pp.85–89; G.L. Gretton, "Missives by Fax or PDF?" (2010) 14 Edin. L.R. 280; R.G Anderson, "Subscription and Settlement by Fax and Email" 2010 S.L.T. (News) 67 and "Fax and Email in Corporate Completions", 2010 S.L.T. (News) 73.

Combined standard clauses for missives have been agreed between Edinburgh and Glasgow—see P. Nicholson, "Clauses Become More Standard" (2009) 54(7) J.L.S. 57; P. Carnan, "For Good Clause" (2009) 54(9) J.L.S. 56; I. Ferguson and P. Carnan, "The New Combined Standard Missives Clauses" (2009) 77 S.L.G. 89; S. Brymer, "The Combined Standard Clauses—A Step in the Right Direction" 2009 Prop. L.B. 102-1—but do not have universal support—M. Smith, "'One Size' is a Dodgy Fit" (2009) 54(12) J.L.S. 54. They have been revised—I.C. Ferguson, "Combined Standard Clauses Version 2—the 2011 Update" (2011) S.L.G. 60.

fn.195. Home Reports are still discussed—J. Scott, "Home Reports Update" (2009) 54(4) J.L.S. 69; (2009) 54(12) J.L.S. 5; P. Nicholson, "Report Card" (2009) 54(12) J.L.S. 12; R. Carswell, (2010) 55(1) J.L.S. 9; (2010) 55(2) J.L.S. 9; correspondence in (2010) 78 S.L.G. 74—and are intended to stay despite the abolition of home information packs in England—"Home Reports to Stay: Minister" (2010) 55(6) J.L.S. 58—but solicitors remain divided on their value. An interim review was published by the Scottish Government on October 1, 2010. The Conveyancing Committee of the Law Society of Scotland issued a critical response in January 2011, available on the Law Society's website *http://www.lawscot.org.uk* [accessed August 23, 2011]. See also *Conveyancing 2010*, pp.84–86.

The Housing (Scotland) Act 2006 (Consequential Provisions) Order 2008 (SI 2008/1889) allows the buyer to rely on the terms of the survey contained in the Home Report; as a consumer protection provision it was outside the legislative competence of the Scottish Parliament.

On supersession of missives see *Aziz v Whannel* [2010] CSOH 136; 2010 **12–59** G.W.D. 33-682; *Conveyancing 2010*, pp.112–114.

On title insurance where there are problems over the soundness of a title or **12–60** other matters see J. Logan, "Risk: Nip it in the Bud" (2009) 54(4) J.L.S. 25; S. Brymer, "Title Insurance—Does More Than It Says on the Tin", 2010 Prop. L.B. 104-5; R. Mannah and S. Brymer, "Title Insurance and the Renewables Industry", 2011 Prop. L.B. 112-5. The SLC *Report on Land Registration*, Pt 26 discusses title insurance, notes that it is useful in non-standard transactions but does not recommend it as a general means of securing title.

12–63 On examination of title see A. Todd, "Examining Titles: A Reminder", 2009 Prop. L.B. 99-7.

12–66 On warrandice from fact and deed granted by an insolvency practitioner disposing of the bankrupt's property see A. Todd and R. Oliphant, "No Guarantees?" (2010) 55(2) J.L.S. 54, suggesting that it may safely be granted, and K. Ross and C. McIntosh, "To Grant or not to Grant?" (2010) 55(4) J.L.S. 56, pointing to dangers in doing so.
  Morris v Rae [2011] CSIH 30; 2011 S.L.T. 701—a party threatening eviction must have an unquestionable title.

12–69 The proposal by the SLC in its *Report on Land Registration*, Pt 14ᵢ to introduce a system of advance notices registered for the benefit of buyers and other grantees to protect them against adverse deeds registered before the buyer's or grantee's own right has been registered, if implemented, could remove the need for letters of obligation as currently used in normal cases and could also have implications for the "offside goals" rule (paras 14.61–14.65 of the Report) which are not fully explored in the Report; S. Brymer, "The Demise of the Letter of Obligation?", 2011 Prop. L.B. 113-1.

12–85 **fn.280.** Under the proposals of the SLC these provisions would be taken out of the body of the new Land Registration Act as being outside its scope but re-enacted in a Schedule.

12–93 In *Hull v Campbell* [2011] CSOH 24; 2011 G.W.D. 5-139 the issue was raised whether a party seeking decree of expiry of the legal title was entitled to obtain ownership of the whole property as adjudged without regard to any disproportion between the value of the property and the amount of the debt or whether (a) under common law the court had a discretion to require the adjudger to account to the debtor for any balance or (b) a decree granting the whole property to the pursuer would be incompatible with the ECHR, art.1, Protocol 1. Lord Turnbull was of the view that, although there was no specific relevant authority, in the light of whole history of adjudication the court had a discretion and also that r.2 of the Protocol applied and so he was not prepared to grant the decree sought by the pursuer, that he was entitled to the whole property. In the light of this indication that he would not obtain decree in the terms which he sought the pursuer moved for dismissal of the action or absolvitor and so the issue was left unresolved.

12–106 **fn.328.** The 2008 Regulations are amended by the Protected Trust Deeds (Scotland) Amendment Regulations 2010 (SSI 2010/398) to deal with secured creditors who have consented to their exclusion.

12–108 **fn.341.** The Bankruptcy (Scotland) Amendment Regulations 2010 (SSI 2010/367) reg.3(5) insert reg.19A into the Bankruptcy (Scotland) Regulations 2008 to provide Form 24 for a notice by the trustee or a trustee acting under a trust deed of proceedings to obtain authority in relation to the debtor's family home under s.40(3A) of the Bankruptcy (Scotland) Act 1985.

12–125 **fn.408.** A consultation has been opened on a proposed increase in prior rights to £470,000 in respect of the house, £29,000 in respect of furniture and cash of £50,000 where there are children and £89,000 where there are none—(2011) 56(3) J.L.S. 34 and 56(6) J.L.S. 28.

fn.410. On s.29 see also *Windram v Windram*, 2009 Fam. L.R. 157; 2009 G.W.D. 36-617 and the critical article by L. Welsh, "Cohabitation Rights" (2010) 55(4) J.L.S. 25, favouring the recommendations of the SLC in its Report on Succession.

fn.413. See also "Symposium. Reform of the Law of Succession" (2010) 14 Edin. L.R. 306; A. Spalding, "People's Choice" (2011) 56(7) J.L.S. 20.

13–03   See the case reported in *The Herald*, noted above, para.**12–03**.

13–05 and   See *Moderator of the General Assembly of the Free Church of Scotland v*
13–09   *Interim Moderator of the Congregation of Strath Free Church of Scotland
(Continuing) (No.2)* [2009] CSOH 113; 2009 S.L.T. 973, following from
Free Church of Scotland (Continuing) v Free Church of Scotland, 2005 S.C.
396 on the right of an owner to have possession of his property and *Moderator
of the Free Church of Scotland v Morrison* [2011] CSIH 52 dealing with a
church held under a specific trust. F. Lyall, "Non-Established Church
Property in Scotland" (2010) 14 Edin. L.R. 113 discusses the broader issue of
ownership of the assets of the Free Church.

13–06   An example of encroachment, with remit to a man of skill to settle the exact
boundary of the land encroached on is *Allen v Thomson*, 2010 S.L.T. (Sh. Ct)
60 and note in *Conveyancing 2010*, pp.44–45.

fn.16. G. Junor, "Acquiescence—And the Singular Successor", 2010 J.R. 217.

13–13   **fn.62.** *Gillies v Ralph* [2008] H.C.J.A.C. 55; 2009 J.C. 25—held that the
established common law powers of entry did not apply in the circumstances
and that it was for the legislature to create new powers; N. Parpworth and K.
Thompson, "Gillies v Ralph: A New Common Law Power of Entry?" 2009
J.R. 209.

13–14   The Protection of Freedoms Bill Pt 3 (ss.39–53) provides for orders made by
statutory instrument repealing unnecessary powers of entry, introducing
additional safeguards in respect of the exercise of such powers and
replacement of powers of entry with new powers, subject to additional
safeguards. In Schs 2 and 10 it repeals a number of powers, but s.45 provides
that these powers may not be exercised in any area within the competence of
the Scottish Parliament.

The procedures for removing and ejection must now take account of the Bankruptcy and Diligence etc. (Scotland) Act 2007 Pt 15 (ss.214–219), brought fully into force from April 4, 2011 by the Bankruptcy and Diligence etc. (Scotland) Act 2007 (Commencement No.8 and Transitional) Order 2011 (SSI 2011/179), made under the 2007 Act s.216(6) as amended by the Housing (Scotland) Act 2010 s.152(3), the AS and the Removing from Heritable Property (Form of Charge) (Scotland) Regulations 2011 (SSI 2011/158); D. Loney, "Removing Hardship?" (2011) 56(7) J.L.S. 48.
14–23 and 14–25

Caution for violent profits may no longer be required although caution for any pecuniary claims remains competent, as the Bankruptcy and Diligence etc. (Scotland) Act 2007 s.219 is brought into force as noted above.
14–29 and 14–60

fn.96. See also *Hamilton v Nairn* [2010] CSIH 77; 2010 S.L.T. 1155; 2011 S.C. 49 at [32].
14–38

See the above case (para.**13–05**) on the owner's right to possession.
14–41

fn.214. *Black v Black*, Unreported June 22, 2010, Dingwall Sh. Ct; affirmed *Black v Black*, 2011 G.W.D. 2-95, Sh. Ct—use of interim orders under s.3(4).
14–70

fn.225. See also the Domestic Abuse (Scotland) Act 2011 (asp 13).
14–73 and 14–88

15–05 *Safraz Mahmood, Petitioner*, 2010 G.W.D. 37-753, Sh. Ct—dispute over whether heritable property was held in partnership or was simply common property.

15–14 and The provisions of the Equality Act 2010 s.37 on adjustments by a disabled
15–17 person to common parts of property in which that person has his or her only or main home may also be noted. The provision is to be expanded by regulations made by the Scottish Ministers and they have launched a consultation on the scope of the Regulations, *The Right to Adapt Common Parts in Scotland*, which concluded on April 1, 2011. Regulations are proposed by the end of the year.

15–18 and Both flats and common areas in developments are often administered by
15–60 factors whose performance of this role has been much criticised. The Property Factors (Scotland) Bill received the Royal Assent on April 7, 2011 as the Property Factors (Scotland) Act 2011 (asp 8). The Act provides in Pt 1 (ss.1–15) for a system of registration of factors and in Pt 2 (ss.16–27) for the introduction of a dispute resolution procedure to improve matters. Part 3 (ss.28–33) in force from April 8, 2011 consists of supplementary provisions which include power to Scottish Ministers to delegate their functions under the Act (s.28). The other provisions of the Act are to be brought into operation by October 1, 2012 at latest (s.33(2)). The first step was taken by the Property Factors (Scotland) Act 2011 (Commencement No.1) Order 2011 (SSI 2011/328) bringing various provisions of the Act into operation from September 23, 2011, some for the purpose of making further regulations or orders (ss.3, 7, 10(5) and 13 (on factors' numbers)).

All factors, as defined in s.2 (now in force) to include land management companies and others paid to maintain common spaces in developments, will require to be registered in a public register, prepared and maintained by the Scottish Ministers (s.1). The criterion for registration is that they are fit and proper persons to act as factors (ss.3–7 partly in force). They will also be required to adhere to a code of conduct prepared by the Scottish Ministers after consultation now opened in terms of the section (s.14). There is provision for removal of unsatisfactory factors from the register, with a right of appeal by summary application to the sheriff (ss.8–11 partly in force) and operating as a factor when unregistered will be an offence (s.12) as well as disentitling the factor from recovering costs and charges or registering a notice of potential liability for costs under the Tenements (Scotland) Act s.13 (s.9). If the Scottish Ministers refuse to register a factor or the factor is removed from the register the relevant owners can also proceed to make new arrangements for factoring (s.9). Section 15 provides for notices and is now in force.

Part 2 provides for the private renting housing panel and committees set up under the Rent Acts to act as the machinery to deal with disputes and designates them as homeowner housing panel and committees respectively when carrying out this function (s.16). Application may be made to the panel where it is alleged that factors are not carrying out their duties or are in breach of the code of conduct (s.17) and if the application is accepted the issue is referred to a homeowner housing committee (s.18) which can issue enforcement orders, which include power to require action to be taken and to make payments, with a right of appeal, but on a point of law only, by summary application to the sheriff (ss.19–22). Failure to conform to an order is reported to the Scottish Ministers (s.23) and constitutes an offence (s.24). There is provision for further regulations (s.25) and for regulations on recovery from factors of costs of applications to the panel and committees (s.26) (both in force).

fn.67. The SLC has now issued a discussion paper on the law of judicial **15–18** factors, *The Law of Judicial Factors* (D.P. No.146, December 2010) reviewing the law and proposing substantial amendments. The Law Society of Scotland will submit a response after consideration of the discussion paper by various committees—(2011) 56(3) J.L.S. 34.

Black v Duncan, 2011 G.W.D. 19-446, Sh.Ct—use of common property **15–19** without consent of co-owner.

On sale of a share of common property to one party in a case under the Family **15–30** Law (Scotland) Act 1985 s.14, see *Adams v Adams*, 2010 S.L.T. (Sh. Ct) 2, discussed in *Conveyancing 2010*, pp.169–170 referring to *Scrimgeour v Scrimgeour* and *Berry v Berry (No.2)* and, probably rightly, favouring the former.

fn.137. On complications arising in a division and sale when one pro indiviso proprietor bid successfully for the property on a sale but failed to pay see *Kinneil v Kinneils* [2010] CSOH 119.

Esposito v Barile, 2010 G.W.D. 23-447, Sh. Ct—claim for unjustified **15–32** enrichment in a dispute over division of the proceeds of sale of common property held in different shares because of initial contribution to the purchase price by one party only; discussed in *Conveyancing 2010*, pp.171–177; K. Swinton, "Unequal Division and Sale" (2010) 78 S.L.G. 86.

fn.152. *Lindsay v Murphy*, 2010 Fam. L.R. 156; 2010 G.W.D. 29-604, Sh. Ct. **15–33**

fn.160. On the burden of proof, held to be on the defender, and on the effect of **15–34** the evidence see *B v B*, 2010 G.W.D. 24-448, commented on by S. Lilley, "A Burden Discharged" (2010) 55(8) J.L.S. 49 and *Conveyancing 2010*, pp.9 and 169.

fn.166. On the Bankruptcy (Scotland) Act 1985 s.40 see *Accountant in Bankruptcy v Clough*, 2010 G.W.D. 35-714, Sh. Ct and *Conveyancing 2010*, pp.10–11. Where the property is jointly owned the trustee is not entitled to warrant to enter into possession or to eject the other co-proprietor— *Stewart's Tr v Stewart*, Unreported September 13, 2011, Peterhead Sh. Ct, referring to *Price v Watson,* 1951 S.C. 359; *Reith v Paterson*, 1993 S.C.L.R. 921 and *Langstane (SP) Housing Association v Davie*, 1994 S.C.L.R. 158.

fn.217; 15–79 fn.299; 15–89 fn.335. *P.S. Properties (2) Ltd v Calloway* **15–52** *Homes Ltd* [2007] CSOH 162; 2007 G.W.D. 31-526 is discussed in R. Rennie, "Counting the Cost in Tenements", 2009 S.L.T. (News) 137.

fn.224. In *Hunter v Tindale*, 2011 S.L.T. (Sh.Ct) 11 it was held that a pend **15–54** leading through a tenement block to a back court was not a "close" in the meaning given to that term by the Tenements (Scotland) Act 2004 s.29(1) and so the owner of the pend was not liable for a share of maintenance costs; discussed in *Conveyancing 2010*, pp.96–97; on appeal Unreported July 22, 2011, Edinburgh Sh. Ct it was held that, although the pend was not a close, the pend was a sector of the tenement and that liability arose under s.8(1) in that the pediment of the archway which required repair provided support; K Swinton, "A Close Decision Pending?" (2011) S.L.G. 61.

15–59 and In *Mehrabadi v Hough*, Unreported January 11, 2010, Aberdeen Sh. Ct
15–71. dormer windows had been added to the roof of a tenement after one defender had obtained title with an obligation to contribute to maintenance of the roof under a real burden in the titles. A second defender had obtained title after the dormer windows were added, with a similar obligation. On appeal, after clarification of the facts, it was held that the first defender was not liable for repairs so far as affecting the windows but the second was. *Conveyancing 2009*, pp.10–11 commenting on the case at first instance suggested that on the facts then found the Tenement Management Scheme should apply to the dormers. The discussion is taken further in *Conveyancing 2010*, pp.93–96 criticising the failure to take account of the Tenements (Scotland) Act 2004— the dormers were scheme property and should have been dealt with under the Tenement Management Scheme or the pursuer could have based his case on ss.8 and 10 of the Act. It might also have been argued that the defender had acquiesced in the addition of the dormers and so was bound under the real burden.

15–69ff On an unsuccessful attempt to adjust liability for burdens by application to the Lands Tribunal for Scotland see *Kennedy v Abbey Lane Properties*, Unreported March 29, 2010, Lands Tr. discussed in *Conveyancing 2010*, pp.97–101 and *Patterson v Drouet*, Unreported January 20, 2011, Lands Tr. discussed in *Conveyancing 2010*, pp.99–102.

fn.261. Lu Xu, "Managing and Maintaining Flatted Buildings: Some Anglo-Scottish Comparisons", 2010 14 Edin. L.R. 236 compares the DMS, TMS and commonhold in England and argues in favour of the DMS.

15–115 The Housing (Scotland) Act 2010 (asp 17) ("the 2010 Act") s.150(1), brought into force by the Housing (Scotland) Act 2010 (Commencement No.2, Transitional, Transitory and Savings Provisions) Order 2011 (SSI 2011/96) from March 1, 2011 amends the Housing (Scotland) Act 2006 (asp 1) ("the 2006 Act") s.50(2)(c)(i) to refer to an owner unwilling as well as one unable to pay.

15–116 The 2010 Act s.150(4), brought into force by the same Order, amends the 2006 Act s.172 on repayment charges to include fees for registration, administrative expenses and interest.

15–149 **fn.489.** The 2010 Act s.150(3), brought into force by the same Order, inserts s.61(3A) into the 2006 Act allowing the local authority to recover from the owner the fee for registration of a maintenance order under s.61(1)(d), any administrative expenses incurred in connection with the registration and interest from the date of demand for payment until payment.

The 2010 Act s.150(2), brought into force by the same Order, amends the 2006 **15–153** Act s.59(1) by adding s.59(1)(aa) to include the expenses of devising a maintenance plan under s.46(1)(b)(ii) or (c) or varying it under s.47(1).

fn.515 and 15–155 fn.520. The provision referred to in **fn.489** also applies to **15–154** registration under s.61(1)(e) of a maintenance plan approved, devised or varied or under s.61(1)(f) of a notice of revocation.

The Crofting Reform (Scotland) Act 2010 (asp 14) s.32 (not yet in force) **15–182** provides for the registration in the new Crofting Register of lands held runrig.

16 fn.1 and 16–20. The SLC has issued a further Discussion Paper on *Accumulation of Income and Lifetime of Private Trusts* (D.P. No.142, January 2010) dealing with the complex question of limitations on accumulation of income first introduced by the Thellusson Act and with the rules on successive liferents. It proposes repeal of the existing provisions and replacement with a new power of the Court of Session to alter the terms of a trust after elapse of a minimum period (of perhaps 25 years). In its Annual Report for 2010 (Scot Law Com No.223) the SLC stated that in 2011 it proposed to issue its Report on Trusts with a new Trusts (Scotland) Bill to replace the Trusts (Scotland) Act 1921 but also to issue a further Discussion Paper on some matters already raised in earlier Discussion Papers.

This *Discussion Paper on Supplementary and Miscellaneous Issues relating to Trust Law* (D.P. No.148, April, 2011) in Pt 1 gives a resume of the work done and seeks views on a proposed comprehensive statutory restatement of trust law, as found in other jurisdictions, in Pt 2 revisits some topics already raised and in Pt 3 suggests measures to expand the range of trusts available, such as private purposes trusts and trusts to hold a controlling interest in a company, as available in other jurisdictions. Comment has been submitted by relevant committees of the Law Society of Scotland—(2011) 56(7) J.L.S. 28.

See also "Symposium:Book X (Trusts) of the DCFR" (2011) 15 Edin. L.R. 462.

16–01 fn.4. The SLC has also issued a discussion paper on the law relating to judicial factors, as noted above, para.**15–18, fn.67**.

16–48 A trust may also be terminated by legislation—Ure Elder Fund Transfer and Dissolution Act 2010 (asp 7). For observations on the Act and the issue of reorganisation of charities see A. Eccles, "Acts of Kindness" (2010) 55(7) J.L.S. 46, mentioning a further Bill, William Simpson's Home (Transfer of · Property etc.) (Scotland) Bill (2010) which became the William Simpson's Home (Transfer of Property etc.) (Scotland) Act 2010 (asp 12).

fn.150. In relation to the reorganisation of charities and restricted funds see the Public Services Reform (Scotland) Act 2010 ss.124 and 125.

fn.2. The Property Standardisation Group has revised its lease management **18–01** documents—"New and Improved" (2010) 55(12) J.L.S. 58.

The *Stair Memorial Encyclopaedia* now deals with crofting in *Stair Memorial Encyclopaedia Reissue* "Crofting" and a new Crofting Reform Bill was put out to consultation—see articles (2009) 54(9) J.L.S. 30; (2010) 55(3) J.L.S. 31; D. Flynn, "Reforming Crofting Law" (2009) 77 S.L.G. 99; A. Nicol and A.G. Fox, "The Future of Crofting" (2010) 55(3) J.L.S. 49. The Bill was passed and was given the Royal Assent on August 6, 2010 as the Crofting Reform (Scotland) Act 2010 (asp 14) (the "2010 Crofting Act"); D. Findlay, "A Future for Crofting" (2010) 55(8) J.L.S. 52.

The 2010 Crofting Act adds considerably to the sea of legislation surrounding the relevant smallholdings but there is promise of consolidation in s.52 which provides for pre-consolidation modification of enactments relating to crofting. The modification is to be made by order of the Scottish Ministers, made once a consolidation Bill has been introduced in the Scottish Parliament and in accordance with the conditions set out in s.53(4)(a), (5) and (6), where such modification would in their opinion facilitate or be otherwise desirable in connection with a consolidation. The Act itself is to be brought into force by commencement orders, apart from s.53 on subordinate legislation, s.54 on ancillary provisions and s.57 on the short title, commencement and Crown application which took effect on August 6, 2010. Consolidation will be all the more welcome in that much of the 2010 Crofting Act is intelligible only with constant reference to the Crofters (Scotland) Act 1993 ("the 1993 Act") quite apart from the amendments which it makes to that Act.

The first steps towards bringing the 2010 Crofting Act into operation are taken by the Crofting Reform (Scotland) Act 2010 (Commencement, Saving and Transitory Provisions) Order 2010 (SSI 2010/437). Despite its title the Order covers only a limited number of provisions noted in the appropriate places below. The savings (art.5) relate to various proceedings begun in or orders made by the Scottish Land Court before the relevant sections come into force and the transitory provision (art.5) provides that references to "the Commission" or "the Crofting Commission" in the Act are to be read as references to the Crofters Commission until that is renamed when the 2010 Crofting Act s.1(1) renaming it the Crofting Commission comes into force as it will do on April 1, 2012 under the Crofting Reform (Scotland) Act 2010 (Commencement No.2, Transitory, Transitional and Saving Provisions) Order 2011 (SSI 2011/334). This Order brings most of the rest of the Act into force either from October 1, 2011 (art.3(1)(a) and Sch. Pt 1) or from April 1, 2012 (art.3(1)(b) and Sch. Pt 2). The main exceptions are the provisions in Pt 2 on registration of crofts, common grazings and lands held runrig and related provisions.

The major changes made by the 2010 Crofting Act are:

(a) Part 1 (ss.1–2), partly in force from October 1, 2011 and fully on April 1, 2012, reorganises the Crofters Commission, renaming it as the Crofting Commission, making new provision on its status, membership, powers, procedures and related matters in Sch.1 and revising and broadening its functions by substituting a new s.1(2) in the 1993 Act and inserting new ss.2A–2D giving the Scottish Ministers powers to modify its functions, requiring an annual report and imposing a duty to produce a plan setting out the Commission's policy to which the Commission itself and the Land Court in considering appeals to it from the Commission must have regard. Consequentially s.1(4) and (5), s.2(2) and (4) and part of s.2(1) of the 1993 Act will be repealed by Sch.4.

(b) Part 2 (ss.3–32), not yet in force, provides for a Crofting Register established and maintained by the Keeper of the Registers of Scotland as a public register of crofts, common grazings and lands held runrig—see note in (2010) 55(9) J.L.S. 15. There is elaborate provision for first registration in s.4 and for registration of events affecting registered crofts in s.5. The persons responsible for applications for registration are set out in s.6, supplemented by the tables in Sch.2. The processing of applications, which must go through the Crofting Commission, which also in some instances can take the initiative, is covered in ss.7–10. Section 11 provides for a registration schedule for registered crofts made up and maintained by the Keeper as a rough equivalent to the title sheet for registered land. First registrations must be notified by the Crofting Commission to interested parties as detailed in s.12 and there is provision for challenge to first registration (s.14), removal of resumed and decrofted crofts from the register (s.15), rectification and indemnity (ss.16–18), rules, fees and appeals (ss.19–20), notification by the Keeper of changes to the registration schedule (s.21) and in ss.22 and 23 consequential changes to ss.3 and 3A of the 1993 Act, inserting a new s.3ZA to provide for registered crofts and s.3AA for the registration of new crofts. The registration of common grazings is covered in ss.24 to 27 and s.28 with Sch.3 applies relevant provisions of the 1993 Act to common grazings. Sections 29 to 31 create offences of failing to make necessary applications for registration and s.32 provides for registration of land held runrig.

(c) Part 3 (ss.33–39), largely in force from October 1, 2011, introduces new duties of crofters and owner-occupier crofters by amendment of the 1993 Act. Section 33 inserts a new s.5AA requiring a crofter to be ordinarily resident on or within 32km of the croft, substitutes a new s.5B imposing a duty not to misuse or neglect the croft and inserts a new s.5C imposing a duty to cultivate the croft or put it to another purposeful use and keep it in a fit state for cultivation so far as compatible with any another purposeful use (all within the terms of the sections). Consequentially sub-ss.5(1A), (2A), (2B) and (7) to (10) of the 1993 Act are repealed by Sch.4.

Section 34 introduces new duties on owner-occupiers of crofts (as defined in s.19B added to the 1993 Act, basically those acquiring from a crofter or from a landlord constituting the croft). The duties, akin to those imposed on crofters, are set out in s.19C and restrictions on division of the croft are set out in s.19D.

Section 35 inserts new ss.21B–21D on consent for absence from the croft granted by the Commission.

Sections 36 and 37 introduce new provisions on enforcement of the duties placed on crofters and owner-occupiers of crofts. Section 36, in force from April 1, 2012, inserts a new s.40A in the 1993 Act requiring the Crofting Commission to give annual notice to them in turn requiring them to give information on whether they are complying with the duties in ss.5AA, 5B, 5C and 19C. Section 37 inserts ss.26A–26K allowing the Commission to investigate suspected breaches of duty reported to them under s.26A and allowing them in any case to take action to enforce the duties, ultimately by termination of a crofter's tenancy (s.26H) or directing an owner-occupier to let the croft (s.26J). Section 26K provides for appeal to the Land Court against decisions of the Commission. Section 38, by inserting a new s.49A in the 1993 Act, imposes on grazings committees a duty to report to the Commission on the condition of the common grazing and the crofts of those sharing it and on any other matters required and on breaches of the duties of crofters and owner-occupiers of crofts.

Section 39, partly in force from October 1, 2011, inserts in the 1993 Act ss.29A and 29B requiring consent of the Commission to letting of an owner-occupied croft (apart from a holiday let of the house or other buildings) and providing that a short lease does not constitute the tenant a crofter or the holder of a 1991 Act tenancy, short limited tenancy or limited duration tenancy within the meaning of the Agricultural Holdings (Scotland) Act 2003.

(d) Part 4 of the Act makes further amendment of various provisions of the 1993 Act, largely in force from October 1, 2011:

(i) Sections 40 and 41 amend ss.13 and 14 on disposal of croft land (see para.**18–111** below).

(ii) Section 42 amends the provisions on resumption of crofts (see para.**18–59** below).

(iii) Section 43 in relation to the Commission's consideration of decrofting directions adds subss.(1A)–(1C) to s.25 to similar effect.

(iv) In relation to the re-letting of crofts subss.44(1) and (2) amend s.11(8)(a) dealing with intestacy to introduce a four-month time limit and by subs.44(6) substitutes a new subs.(5A) in s.23 to deal with failure of the landlord to make any proposal or an acceptable proposal within the four months where the vacancy arises on intestacy. Subsections 44(3)–(5), dealing with vacant crofts generally, amends subs.23(5) to introduce a two-month time limit and repeal the words from "and if" to the end and adds subss.(5ZA)–(5ZC) on proposals to let the croft, distinguishing in time limits between a vacancy arising on intestacy under s.11(8) and other cases.

(v) Section 45 inserts subs.24(3A) to allow the Commission to disregard an application by the landlord to decroft where action is being taken to re-let the croft under ss.11(8)(a), 23(5) or 23(5B) and (5C).

(vi) Section 46 substitutes a new s.4 on enlargement of crofts taking account of registration requirements.

(vii) Section 47 substitutes a new s.51 on enlargement of common grazings likewise taking account of registration requirements.

(viii) Section 48, in force from April 1, 2012, amends substantially s.58A on obtaining Commission approval or consent and adds s.58B allowing variation of conditions imposed on an approval or consent.

(ix) Section 49 amends substantially s.10 on bequest of crofts (see para.**18–44** below).

(x) Section 50(1) (brought into force with savings by the Commencement Order, arts 3 and 5(3)) removes references to appeal by way of stated case in appeals under ss.25(8), 38A(1) and 52A(2)(a) and s.50(2), force from October 1, 2011, inserts s.52A(4B) allowing the Commission to be party to an appeal or proceedings before the Land Court on an application under s.53(1).

(xi) Part 5 of the Act (ss.51–57) is the general and miscellaneous part providing in s.51 for a duty on the Scottish Ministers to lay a quadriennial report on crofting before the Scottish Parliament (brought into force from December 22, 2010 by the Commencement Order art.3), in s.52 for pre-consolidation modification of crofting enactments, in ss.53 and 54 for subordinate legislation and ancillary provisions, in s.56 (also in force from December 22, 2010 under the above Commencement Order) for the interpretation provisions and in s.57 for the short title, commencement by order and application as binding on the Crown. Section 55 (brought partially into force from December 22, 2010 by the first Commencement Order and more fully by the second Commencement Order, see D. Findlay, "Crofting Briefing", Journal Online, October 2011, *www.journalonline.co.uk* [accessed October 25, 2011]) provides for the consequential amendments and repeals in Sch.4 relating to the Small Landholders (Scotland) Act 1911 (inserting references to the Crofters Commission for the Board), the Succession (Scotland) Act 1964 s.16 (to deal specially with crofting leases), the 1993 Act (additional to those in the body of the Act) and the Ethical Standards in Public Life etc. (Scotland) Act 2000 Sch.3 (to substitute "Crofting" for "Crofters" Commission). In the case of the 1993 Act the list of amendments and repeals is very substantial, running to 14 printed pages; many take account of the new provisions on registration of crofts when they come in force and are intended to ensure that application for registration is made as required or that an action or event, such as assignation or division of a croft is duly registered by nullifying consents or other actions if the appropriate registration is not applied for and making the date of registration the effective date; there is also a new s.60 on regulations and orders and additional interpretation provisions. These amendments mean that the 2010 Act must always be consulted along with the 1993 Act.

On agricultural tenancies a fourth edition of Lord Gill's *Agricultural Tenancies* is in the works, but the date of publication is not yet settled. S.M. Notley, *Handbook on Scottish Agricultural Law* (Avizandum Publishing Ltd, 2009) is also relevant to agricultural tenancies. The Scottish Government initiated a consultation on reduction or removal of burdens on landlords and tenants arising from the Agricultural Holdings (Scotland) Acts of 1991 and 2003—*www.scotland.gov.uk/Resource/Doc/327812/0105898.pdf* [accessed August 24, 2011]—and amendments to the Act, which do not include all those agreed by the Tenant Farming Forum which was consulted, are set out in the Public Services Reform (Agricultural Holdings) (Scotland) Order 2011 (SSI 2011/232) made under the Public Services Reform (Scotland) Act 2010 s.17 as a first use of the powers given in that section—see the critical comment on the draft of the Order by A.G. Fox, "Creating a Jigsaw" (2010) 55(12) J.L.S. 49. The draft was also criticised by the Rural Affairs Sub-Committee of the Law Society of Scotland particularly for the omission to accept the suggestions of the Tenant Farming Forum to widen the class of beneficiaries succeeding to a tenancy as near relatives in the 1991 Act s.25 and Sch.2 to include a grandchild and to amend the provisions on rent review to prohibit "upward only" rent reviews and "landlord only initiated" reviews— "Law Reform Update" (2011) 56(2) J.L.S. 33; see also K.R. Mackay, "Further Agricultural Holdings Legislation", 2011 Prop. L.B. 111-7. The changes made are noted at the appropriate points below in paras **18–46, 18– 96** and **18–179**. However, proposals for an Agricultural Holdings (Amendment) (Scotland) Bill to make good these omissions and to deal with the unintended adverse effects on rent reviews resulting from the decision in *Mason v Boscawen* [2008] EWHC 3100 (Ch), that VAT is part of the rent, which were already removed for English law by the Finance Act 2009 s.79, but might still apply in Scotland if the decision was followed, were put out to consultation in March 22, 2011—see paras **18–46** and **18–179**. They are included in new legislation.

On leases generally, a fourth edition of A. McAllister, *The Scottish Law of Leases* is due in December, 2011. On commercial leases a second edition of D. Cockburn, *Commercial Leases*, by D. Cockburn and R. Mitchell, was published in September, 2011 and on housing law P. Robson, *Housing Law* (Dundee University Press) was published in February, 2011. See also *Stair Memorial Encyclopaedia Reissue* "Landlord and Tenant".

L.A. Faichnie, "Changes to Fair" (2009) 54(4) J.L.S. 67 analyses changes in practice in drawing commercial leases to take account of economic problems, new legislation on carbon emissions and "green" leases.

In relation to leases of special subjects attention is drawn to the potential adverse taxation consequences of using a long lease as the medium for a renewable energy contract by C. Whittle, S. Mathieson and J. Whittle, "It's an Ill Wind ... " (2011) 56(4) J.L.S. 55.

Commercial leases are often extremely complex and dealing with them often **18–02** leads to issues of interpretation—see, e.g. *Multilink Leisure Developments Ltd v North Lanarkshire Council* [2010] CSOH 114; 2009 S.L.T. 1170; reversed [2009] CSIH 46; 2010 S.C. 302; [2010] UKSC 47; 2011 S.L.T. 184; 2011 U.K.S.C 53 (noted further below **18–108, fn.474**); *Landmore Ltd v Shanks Dumfries and Galloway Ltd* [2011] CSOH 100. On the meaning of the expression "use all reasonable endeavours" to pursue a development project involving assignation and re-assignation of leases see *EDI Central Ltd v National Car Parks Ltd* [2010] CSOH 141; 2011 S.L.T. 75 see also more generally on this expression the cases and discussions referred to above in para.**12–57**; *R & D Construction Group Ltd v Hallam Land Management Ltd* [2010] CSIH 96; 2011 S.L.T. 326; 2011 S.C. 286; G. Junor, "Agreement to Agree—With All Reasonable Endeavours" 2009 Prop. L.B.102-4 and case commentary 2011 S.L.T. (News) 61; *Conveyancing 2010*, pp.104–112.

On interpretation generally, an issue which frequently arises in leases and other contracts relating to land, see the SLC *Discussion Paper on Review of Contract Law: Interpretation of Contracts* (D.P. No.147, February 2011). D. Cabrelli, "Interpretation of Contracts, Objectivity and the Elision of the Significance of Consent Achieved through Concession and Compromise", 2011 J.R. 121; M. Hogg, "Fundamental Issues for the Reform of the Law of Contractual Interpretation" (2011) 15 Edin. L.R. 406.

The 20-year restriction on residential leases is removed for lessees who are **18–03** social landlords (within the meaning of the Housing (Scotland) Act 2010 s.165), or bodies connected to a social landlord (within the meaning of that Act s.164) or rural housing bodies (within the meaning of the Title Conditions (Scotland) Act 2003 s.122(1) by the 2010 Housing Act s.138, which amends the Land Tenure Reform (Scotland) Act 1974 by adding s.8(3A). Further changes are made by the Private Rented Housing (Scotland) Act 2011 (asp 14) as noted in para.**18–09, fn.7** below.

A fundamental requirement of a lease, as of other contracts, is that the object, **18–05** in this case the use granted, should be lawful—see *Robert Purvis Plant Hire Ltd v Brewster* [2009] CSOH 28; 2009 Hous. L.R. 34 noted in 2009 Prop. L.B. 100-8 primarily dealing with frustration of the contract.

fn.7. That the 20-year limit on residential leases might be altered was **18–09** mentioned in the consultation mentioned in **fn.9** below. It has been altered to a limited extent in another context as noted above in para.**18–03** and the Private Rented Housing (Scotland) Act 2011 (asp 14), brought partially into force from August 31, 2011 by the Private Rented Housing Act 2011 (Commencement No.1 and Saving Provision) Order 2011 (SSI 2011/270)

("the first Commencement Order"), by s.36(2) and (3), which amend the Land
Tenure Reform (Scotland) Act 1974 s.8, makes more general provision for a
lease to a body prescribed or of a type prescribed by the Scottish Ministers by
order made by statutory instrument (s.8(3A)(d)), laid before and approved by
resolution of the Scottish Parliament (s.8(3D)). Details of the circumstances
for which an order may provide are set out in the new s.8(3B) and (3C), the
latter allowing provision for protection of tenants or occupiers of dwelling-
houses in the property.

fn.9. The draft bill to implement the SLC *Report on Conversion of Long
Leases* was put out to consultation in May 2010. On the response of the Law
Society of Scotland's Conveyancing Committee see (2010) 55(7) J.L.S. 31 and
on the Bill itself, para.**18–105** below.

18–06 **fn.14 and 18–10.** The Property Standardisation Group has produced a form of
licence to occupy retail or office premises, with guidance notes.

18–12 The references to legislation against discrimination should now be to the
Equality Acts 2006 and 2010.
  In *Crewpace Ltd v French* [2011] CSOH 133 it was held that where there
was a single lease of two separate properties but the rent had been
apportioned between the two landowners/landlords one landlord had no
interest to object to transactions affecting the land of the other; there was no
"joint landlord's interest".

fn.37. A case on misrepresentation, *Cramaso LLP v Viscount Reidhaven's Trs*
[2010] CSOH 62; 2010 G.W.D. 20-403, brings out the importance of
identifying the parties to a lease, the lease in this case having been granted to
a party (an LLP) different from the party who negotiated it.

fn.39. On the 2003 Act ss.70–72 see *Salvesen v Riddell SLC/3/09*, July 29,
2010 commented on by A.G. Fox and F.M. Stephen, "Courting
Controversy" (2010) 55(9) J.L.S. 50, 51.

fn.41. The system of private landlord registration will be further amended by
the Private Rented Housing (Scotland) Act 2011 (asp 14). The amendments are
made in Pt 1 of the Act (ss.1–12). Section 1 will amend the Antisocial
Behaviour (Scotland) Act 2004 s.85 to add further specification of
considerations affecting whether a landlord is a fit and proper person; s.2,
brought into force from August 31, 2011 by the first Commencement Order
(the Private Rented Housing (Scotland) Act 2011 (Commencement No.1 and
Saving Provision) Order 2011 (SSI 2011/270)), adds s.85A allowing local
authorities to require a criminal record certificate; s.3 will amend ss.84 and 86
on landlord registration numbers in the register while s.6 will insert s.92B
requiring the landlord registration number in advertisements; s.4, brought
partly into force on August 31, 2011 to enable regulations to be made,
amends s.88 on appointment of agents; s.5 will add provisions in s.88A on
access to the register and a new s.92ZA imposing a duty to note refusals and
removals in the register; s.7, brought into force from August 31, 2011, with a
saving provision for offences committed before that date, changes the penalty
in s.93(7) to £50,000; s.8 will add s.93A allowing a court to impose a
disqualification order for up to five years for breach of s.93(1) or (2); s.9 will
add ss.97A and 97B giving local authorities power to obtain information

about any house in its area to enable or assist it in exercising its functions under the Act; s.10, brought into force from August 31, 2011, adds s.99A to the 2004 Act requiring local authorities to have regard to guidance issued by the Scottish Ministers in exercising their powers; s.11 will insert s.22A in the Housing (Scotland) Act 2006 requiring private rented housing panels to give local authorities information on details of the house concerned to maintain the register under s.82(1) of the 2004 Act; s.12 introduces the Schedule with consequential modifications to the 2004 Act.

A working group was set up to develop a voluntary accreditation scheme for property managers in the light of complaints over the performance of factors—(2010) 55(6) J.L.S. 58, *Conveyancing 2010*, pp.65–66. However the Property Factors (Scotland) Act 2011 noted in paras **15–18** and **15–60** provides for compulsory registration.

fn.42. The provisions on licensing of HMOs in the Housing (Scotland) Act 2006 (Pt 5 ss.124–166) were brought into force as from August 31, 2010 by the Housing (Scotland) Act 2006 (Commencement No.8, Transitional Provisions and Savings) Order 2010 (SSI 2010/159) art.3, but further amendments are made in the Private Rented Housing (Scotland) Act 2011 referred to in **fn.41** above; s.13(1) of this Act, brought into force from August 31, 2011 by the first Commencement Order, amends the Housing (Scotland) Act 2006 s.125(1) to bring also within the regime living accommodation of such type or which is occupied in such manner as the Scottish Ministers may by order specify, and adds s.125(1A) requiring the Scottish Ministers to consult local authorities and such tenants or their representatives and such landlords or their representatives as they think fit before making an order; it also repeals s.125(4)(a); s.13(2) will insert s.129A into the 2006 Act, allowing a local authority to refuse to consider an application for an HMO licence if it considers that occupation of the living accommodation would breach planning control; s.13(3), in force from August 31, 3011, inserts subss.(da) and (db) in s.131 of the 2006 Act referring to subdivision or adaptation of rooms; s.13(4) will insert s.131A in the 2006 Act allowing a local authority to refuse an HMO licence to avoid over-provision of HMOs in a locality with consequent amendment of ss.135 and 191(4)(a), the latter amended by the 2011 Act s.13(6) as from August 31, 2011; s.14, in force from August 31, 2011, increases the penalty in s.156(1)(a) to £50,000; s.15, also in force from that date, amends s.158(12)(a) of the 2006 Act to replace the duty to give reasons for a decision with a duty to advise of a right to request reasons as provided for in new subss.(13) to (17), with consequent addition of s.159(5A) on appeals, providing that a sheriff may require a local authority to give reasons for its decision if it has not already done so; s.16, also in force from August 31, 2011, adds a reference to s.186 in s.163(1) on guidance of which a draft has been published; Pt 3 of the Bill (ss.17–31) has partly related provisions on new overcrowding statutory notices requiring landlords to avoid overcrowding.

S. Grant and L. Black, "Advice on HMO Legislation", 2010 Prop. L.B.106-8.

Them Properties LLP v Glasgow City Council [2010] CSIH 51; 2010 Hous. L.R. 69—appeal against refusal of an HMO licence, discussed in *Conveyancing 2010*, pp.180–182; *Thomson v Aberdeen City Council*, 2011 G.W.D. 12-283, Sh. Ct—appeal on refusal of HMO licence rejected where the applicant had attempted to evade the requirements and set up false claims.

fn.75. *Coatbridge Retail No.11 Ltd v Oliver*, 2010 G.W.D. 19-374, Sh. Ct. **18–21**

18–26 and   See the new provisions on removing noted in paras **14–23** and **14–25** above.
18–27

18–28   **fn.106.** On assignation of crofts see *Stair Memorial Encyclopaedia Reissue* "Crofting", para.54. The Crofting Act 2010 Sch.4, para.3(8), partially in force from October 1, 2011, amends the 1993 Act s.8 adding new subss.(1A) and (1B), repealing subs.(2), amending subs.(6) and adding subs.(6A) so as to require additional information, in particular information on the residence of the proposed assignee, an application for registration of an unregistered croft and putting a three-month time limit on a consent to assign a registered croft unless an application for registration is made within that period. The assignation takes effect on the date of registration. The provisions on registration are not yet in force.

    fn.106. On assignation of an agricultural holding to a person entitled on intestacy under the Agricultural Holdings (Scotland) Act 1991 s.10A see *Fleming v Ladykirk Estates Ltd SLC/62/08*; 2009 S.C.L.R. 28 commented on by A.G. Fox, "Win Some, Lose Some" (2009) 54(6) J.L.S. 50.

18–30   **fn.115.** *Credential Bath St Ltd v DLA Piper Scotland LLP* [2010] CSOH 26; 2010 G.W.D. 17-347—on step-in provisions in a guarantee and solicitors' responsibility.

18–33   **fn.133.** On assignation of crofts see *Stair Memorial Encyclopaedia Reissue* "Crofting", para.54 and para.**18–28** above.

18–35   On subletting of crofts see *Stair Memorial Encyclopaedia Reissue* "Crofting", para.55. Under the Crofting Act 2010 Sch.4 para.3(18), in force from October 1, 2011, the 1993 Act s.27(3) is repealed.

    fn.135. A. Todd, "Drafting Sub-leases of Part", 2009 Prop. L.B. 98-1.

18–41   **fn.156.** *Primary Healthcare Centres (Broadford) Ltd v Humphrey* [2010] CSOH 129; 2010 G.W.D. 35-730 carries the litigation in [2009] CSOH 46; 2009 S.L.T. 673 on liability of the partners further, with [2011] CSOH 92 on expenses.

18–44   On bequest of crofts see *Stair Memorial Encyclopaedia Reissue* "Crofting", paras 81–82. The Crofting Act 2010 s.49, in force from October 1, 2011, amends s.10(1) of the 1993 Act to allow bequest of the whole tenancy to one natural person or to two or more natural persons who together would succeed the crofter as tenant of the whole croft, substitutes a new s.10(2) requiring a legatee who accepts the bequest to give notice to the landlord, with a copy to the Crofting Commission, within 12 months of the crofter's death, substitutes for subss.(2B) to (4D) new subss.(3), (4) and (4A) to (4C)(a) (consent to division under the 1993 Act, s.9), amends subs.(4E) to add reference to a new subs.(4EA) and inserts new subss.(7) and (8) taking account of possible division of the croft where there is more than one legatee and provisions on possible registration are not yet in force.

    In bequests of leases there are critical dates for giving notice to the landlord which, if overlooked, give rise to claims under the Law Society of Scotland's Master Policy—(2010) 55(7) J.L.S. 36.

Forbes v Cameron [2010] CSIH 25; 2010 S.L.T. 1017—meaning of **18–46**
"Whitsunday" in relation to the date of service of a notice determined as May
28 by the Term and Quarter Days (Scotland) Act 1990 in absence of clear
indication otherwise in the lease.

The Public Services Reform (Agricultural Holdings) (Scotland) Order 2011
(SSI 2011/232) ("the Agricultural Holdings Order") art.3 amends the
Agricultural Holdings (Scotland) Act 1991 Sch.2 to refer to a "viable unit"
meaning one which in the opinion of the Land Court offers full-time
employment and the means to pay the rent and maintain the holding
adequately.

The proposed Agricultural Holdings (Amendment) (Scotland) Bill
included in the Scottish Government's legislative programme for 2011–2012
will amend the term "near relative" in the 1991 Act s.25 and Sch.2 to include
grandchildren; A. Fox and D. Reid, "The Colour Yellow" (2011) 56(6) J.L.S.
44 on this and other possible changes on farming-related matters; C. Clark,
"Farm Tenancies; More Changes Imminent" (2011) 56(6) J.L.S. 57 on this
and the other changes proposed.

On bequest of crofts see *Stair Memorial Encyclopaedia Reissue* "Crofting", **18–48**
paras 81–82 and the 2010 Crofting Act (see para.**18–44** above).

fn.184. Nomination of a proposed transferee is not enough to transfer the **18–52**
tenancy; there must be an act of transfer by the executor and if the executor is
not yet confirmed the confirmation must be obtained within a year of the
death—*McGrath v Nelson* [2010] CSOH 149; 2011 S.L.T. 107, following
Garvie's Trs v Garvie's Tutors, 1975 S.L.T. 94.

fn.185. On intestate succession to crofts see *Stair Memorial Encyclopaedia
Reissue* "Crofting", paras 83–85. The Crofting Act 2010 s.44(1) and (2) and
Sch.4, para.3(10), largely in force from October 1, 2011, amend s.11(1) to
require the executor to give notice to the landlord with a copy to the Crofting
Commission; add subs.(1A) on registration (not yet in force); substitute "24"
for "12" in subs.(2) and refer to giving the landlord notice; substitute "10" for
"10(2)" in subs.(3) and repeal para.(d); substitute "24" for "12" in subs.(4) and
refer to giving the landlord notice and insert in subs.(8)(a) after "them"
"before the expiry of the period of four months beginning with the day on
which the notice is given" while also substituting a new subs.(5A) in s.23
dealing with the case where a croft is declared vacant under s.11(8).

fn.206. *Coatbridge Retail No.1 Ltd v Oliver*, 2010 G.W.D. 19-374, Sh. Ct. **18–55**

fn.209. On giving notice to the correct party see *AWD Chase de Vere Wealth
Management Ltd v Melville Street Properties Ltd* [2009] CSOH 150; 2010
S.C.L.R. 521 and *Batt Cables plc v Spencer Business Parks Ltd* [2010] CSOH
81; 2010 S.L.T. 860.

Advice on risk management issues in relation to break clauses is offered by
L. Kerr, "Breaking Up is Hard to Do" (2009) 54(9) J.L.S. 42; errors in giving
effect to break clauses are a major source of claims under the Law Society of
Scotland's Master Policy—(2009) 54(12) J.L.S. 41; (2010) 55(7) J.L.S. 36.

fn.230. The Crofting Act 2010 s.42, in force from October 1, 2011, after **18–59**
s.20(1A) of the 1993 Act adds subss.(1AA) to (1AD) extending the discretion
of the Land Court to decide whether it is satisfied that the landlord's purpose is

reasonable to take into account sustainability of crofting and the crofting community, the landscape and the environment and the social and cultural benefits associated with crofting.

18–61 On renunciation of crofting tenancies see *Stair Memorial Encyclopaedia Reissue* "Crofting", para.57.

18–63 **fn.243 and 18–68.** On tenant's breach of obligations sufficiently material to justify rescission see *Crieff Highland Gathering Ltd v Perth and Kinross Council* [2011] CSOH 78; 2011 G.W.D. 20-474, esp. at paras [42] et seq. referring, in relation to rescission, to the article by M.A. Hogg and holding that the authorities indicate that rescission has regard to the tenant's future conduct.

18–66 **fn.266.** In *Kodak Processing Companies Ltd v Shoredale Ltd* [2009] CSIH 71; 2010 S.C. 113; 2009 S.L.T. 1151, noted in 2009 Prop. L.B. 103-7, it was held as a matter of what seems dubious statutory construction that the service by recorded delivery required under the 1985 Act s.4(2) was service using the service under that name operated by the Post Office and that delivery by a sheriff officer alone was incompetent even during a postal strike; commented on by L. Richmond, "Signed, Sealed and ... Delivered?", 2010 S.L.T. (News) 63.

fn.267 and fn.268. See *Crieff Highland Gathering Ltd v Perth and Kinross Council* [2010] CSOH 67; 2010 G.W.D. 22-431—proof before answer and after proof [2011] CSOH 78; 2011 G.W.D. 20-474, esp. at paras [55] et seq. holding that insufficient time had been given to obtemper the requirements and that a fair and reasonable landlord would not in the circumstances have sought irritancy or rescission of the lease.

18–80 The Private Rented Housing (Scotland) Act 2011 s.34, brought into force from August 31, 2011 by the first Commencement Order, amends the 1988 Act s.33 adding subs.(5) to provide that, for avoidance of doubt, ss.18 and 19 do not apply for the purpose of a landlord seeking to recover possession under s.33.

18–87 The Housing (Scotland) Act 2010 s.154, brought into force from March 1, 2011 by the Housing (Scotland) Act 2010 (Commencement No.2, Transitional, Transitory and Saving Provisions) Order 2011 (SSI 2011/96), amends the Housing (Scotland) Act 2001 Sch.1, para.2 to provide that a tenancy is not a Scottish secure tenancy if the landlord is a local authority and the house is held for the purposes of a police force or expressly temporarily let pending its requirement for a police force, with exceptions for cases arising before March 1, 2011.

fn.383. In *Cochrane v Grampian Joint Police Board*, 2010 S.L.T. (Lands Tr.) 19; 2010 Hous. L.R. 57, the Tribunal, observing that it was not bound to follow previous decisions, held that a police constable was not in the circumstances a secure tenant, and did not follow *Robb v Tayside Joint Police Board*, 2009 S.L.T. (Lands Tr.) 23.

18–88 Communities Scotland was replaced by the Scottish Housing Regulator as an executive agency of Scottish Ministers in 2008 (see para.**25–32**) and, although one of the purposes of the Housing (Scotland) Act 2010 is to limit the scope of the right to buy scheme, the main thrust of the Act is to introduce a new scheme of regulation of "social landlords" as defined, namely social landlords to be registered under ss.22–26 of the Act and for the time being those already registered under the Housing (Scotland) Act 2001 s.57, local authority landlords and local authorities providing housing services for the homeless and others (s.165). For this purpose the Scottish Housing Regulator is converted into a statutory corporate body independent of Ministers (s.7), responsible for registration of social landlords other than local authorities and for oversight of the performance of all social landlords, and much of the Act is concerned with setting out its powers and duties. The Act is being brought into force in stages with the first main commencement order being the Housing (Scotland) Act 2010 (Commencement No.2, Transitional, Transitory and Saving Provisions) Order 2011 (SSI 2011/96) setting various commencement dates for different provisions of the Act in art.2 and its Schedule.

Part 1 of the Act (ss.1–19 and Sch.1) sets up the Regulator and sets out its various powers and obligations, including obligations to consult on such matters as guidance and codes of practice (for which purpose other sections noted below are also brought into force). It came partially into force on April 1, 2011 under SSI 2011/96. In Pt 2 of the Act (ss.22–30), dealing with registered social landlords, s.24. which sets out the legislative criteria for registration, e.g. that they should not trade for profit and should carry on housing activities in Scotland, comes into force on that day but only for the purpose of allowing Ministers to make orders adapting the Act to registered social landlords which are not registered societies or companies, while ss.25, 26 and 28 on regulatory criteria and voluntary deregistration are brought into force only for the purpose of allowing the Regulator to enter into consultations. In Pt 3 (ss.31–41), dealing with performance by social landlords, ss.31–33 on the Scottish social housing charter covering the standards and outcomes to be achieved by social landlords in performing their housing activities and s.39 on encouraging equal opportunities came into force on April 1, 2011 under SSI 2011/96, while s.35 on guidance generally and s.36 on a code of conduct on governance and financial accountability for registered social landlords have been brought into force for the purpose of allowing consultation by the Regulator. A consultation on a draft Scottish Social Housing Charter closes in October. In Pt 4 (ss.42–51), on the inquiries and information which the Regulator may make and seek and its powers in those respects, s.46(2) on the types of inquiries on which a report will be made to Scottish Ministers and others and s.47(2) on what the Regulator considers to be significant performance failures on which tenants may provide information came into force on April 1, 2011, while ss.50 and 51 on guidance and a code of practice came into force only for the purpose of allowing consultation by the Regulator.

Part 5 (ss.52–67) deals with regulatory intervention and wide powers are given to the Regulator to intervene in order to improve performance by social landlords, e.g. by requiring a performance improvement plan, appointing managers and removing officers of registered social landlords but only s.54 on a code of practice on exercise of the Regulator's powers has been brought into force from April 1, 2011 by SSI 2011/96 and that for consultation only. Again, in Pt 6 (ss.68–72), on the accounts and audit of accounts of registered social landlords, only s.68, on defining the accounting requirements, was brought into force from April 1, 2011 and that for consultation only. Likewise in Pt 7 (ss.73–91), dealing with issues of insolvency and containing extensive powers of intervention by the Regulator including moratoria on debts and control over enforcement of security rights, only s.73(3) on consultation over notification of steps to be taken to enforce a security right was brought into force from April 1, 2011. Part 8 (ss.92–106) on organisational change in registered social landlords, ranging from change of name to restructuring, is not in force and in Pt 9 (ss.107–112), dealing with disposal of the land or other assets of registered social landlords and generally requiring the consent of the Regulator except for such cases as grant of a secure, assured or short assured tenancy, only s.108(3) and s.109(4) providing for consultation by the Regulator were brought into force, again from April 1, 2011 under SSI 2011/ 96.

Part 10 (ss.113–124) dealing with the special procedures required where disposals (Ch.1 ss.113–121) or restructuring (Ch.2 ss.123–124) of registered social landlords result in a change of landlord with potential prejudice to tenants is not in force, nor is Pt 11 (ss.125–136), headed "Change of landlord: secure tenants", which sets out the procedure for acquisition by "approved persons" with consent of the Regulator of houses held from local authority landlords on secure tenancies. The procedure is similar to acquisition under the right to buy. Part 12 (s.137) makes provision for charitable registered social landlords entered in the Scottish Charity Register. Parts 13 (ss.138 and 139), 14 (ss.140–147), 15 (ss.148–151) and 16 (ss.152–158) are largely in force and are dealt with at appropriate points elsewhere so far as relevant to the present work. In Pt 17 (ss.159–167), the supplementary and final provisions, ss.161, 163 and 165–167 came into force on Royal Assent as being the usual formal provisions on orders etc. and interpretation. Section 159 provides that individuals consenting to or conniving at offences by corporate bodies are also liable; s.160 defines "formal communications", which are to be in writing, and their delivery; s.162 provides for minor amendments and repeals detailed in Sch.2 and of these para.2 was brought into force from March 1, 2011 and paras 6, 8, 9 and 10 from April 1, 2011 by SSI 2011/96. The definition of "connected bodies" in s.164 and Sch.2 para.2, relevant to ss.138 and 139, which disapply the normal limitations on the length of leases and redemption of security rights in the case of social landlords (see paras **18–87, 124, 125, 129** and the relevant pages of Ch.21), was brought into force from March 1, 2011, again by SSI 2011/96.

fn.387. *South Lanarkshire Council v McKenna*, 2010 Hous. L.R. 36; 2010 G.W.D. 20-401, Sh. Ct—in terms of the Housing (Scotland) Act 2001 ss.34 and 35 a short Scottish secure tenancy must be for a minimum of six months whether it is created initially or is converted from a Scottish secure tenancy.

18–89 On abandonment in terms of s.17 of the Housing (Scotland) Act 2001 and recovery of possession using s.18 see *Lech v Highland Council*, 2010 Hous. L.R. 52; 2010 G.W.D. 24-506, Sh. Ct.

The Housing (Scotland) Act 2010 s.153, brought into force by the Housing (Scotland) Act 2010 (Commencement No.3) Order 2011 (SSI 2011/181) but only for the purpose of allowing consultation by the Scottish Ministers under the Housing (Scotland) Act 2001 s.16(5B), adds subss.16(5A) and 16(5B) to the Housing (Scotland) Act 2001, to give additional protection to tenants when re-possession is sought on a ground consisting of or including non-payment of rent; s.155 (not yet in force) by amendment of s.14, including the addition of subs.(2A), and addition of a new s.14A, introduces an elaborate set of pre-action requirements where proceedings are to be based on non-payment of rent, including such matters as providing advice on housing benefit or other financial assistance and assistance on debt-management and attempts to work out a payments plan.

fn.392. *Campbell v Glasgow Housing Association* [2009] CSOH 154; 2010 S.L.T. 274—no waiver of proceedings for recovery of property simply by receipt of payment of rent before decree can take effect. A later attempt by Mr Campbell to reduce the decree of ejection granted against him in September, 2009 failed—*Campbell v Glasgow Housing Association* [2011] CSOH 55; 2011 G.W.D. 13-306; L. McDermid, "Recovery of Possession—Protection for Vulnerable Tenants" (2011) 79 S.L.T. 63, referring also to the proposed changes in the 2010 Act. On the possible relevance of art.8 of the E.C.H.R. see G. Junor, "A Pinnock Defence in Scotland?", 2011 S.L.T. (News) 45.

G. Junor, "Can We Keep the Shop? Invoking the Tenancy of Shops (Scotland)   **18–90**
Act 1949", 2009 Prop. L.B. 98-5.

Loudon v Hamilton [2010] CSIH 36; 2010 S.L.T. 984; 2011 S.C. 255—the   **18–93**
Agricultural Holdings (Scotland) Act 1991 s.2(2)(c) excludes from protection as an agricultural holding grazing lets for less than a year but the period of less than a year need not be exactly defined if it can be inferred that lets were for less than a year at a time.

It was observed that because interdict could cause significant financial loss if not justified the Land Court should grant interim interdict only in a real emergency and after hearing submissions; notice should be given if there was no emergency; averments should be tested rigorously; and caution should be considered.

The case is commented on by A.G. Fox and F.M. Stephen, "Courting Controversy" (2010) 55(9) J.L.S. 50.

fn.422. A.G. Fox, "Win Some, Lose Some" (2009) 54(6) J.L.S. 50 comments   **18–95**
on *Trs of North Berwick Trust*.

The Agricultural Holdings Order 2011 art.7 amends the Agricultural Holdings   **18–96**
(Scotland) Act 2003 ss.5 and 8(6) to reduce the length of a limited duration tenancy from 15 to 10 years and art.8 substitutes a new s.5(2) allowing conversion of a short limited duration tenancy to a limited duration tenancy by written agreement entered into before expiry of the short limited duration tenancy.

On the definition of crofts and the changes made by the 2007 Act referred to in   **18–97**
fn.435 see *Stair Memorial Encyclopaedia Reissue* "Crofting", paras 23–28; 30–36; 43–56; 86–92; 110–113; 122–129.

The Crofting (Designation of Areas) (Scotland) Order 2010 (SSI 2010/29), made under the 1993 Act s.3A(1)(b), extends to areas adjacent to the present crofting counties specified in the Order the areas in which the Crofters Commission can constitute a croft on application by the owner of the land under s.41 of the Act.

See *Stair Memorial Encyclopaedia Reissue* "Crofting", paras 94–99. On the   **18–98**
procedure for ejection see the provisions noted in paras **14–23** and **14–25** above.

fn.443. *MacColl v Crofters Commission and MacGillivray* [2009] CSOH 120; 2010 S.L.T. 128—arrangement held to be a genuine lease to the second defender (to which consent was given by the Commission under the 1993 Act s.23) and not a purchase.

18–103 *Appeal by A. Cartledge under the Town and Country Planning (Scotland) Act 1997 s.239* [2010] CSOH 46; 2010 G.W.D. 16-323—planning permission and site licences overlap but the number of caravans permitted by planning permission can be controlled by the site licence; on appeal *Cartledge v The Scottish Ministers* [2011] CSIH 23; 2011 S.L.T. 787 it was held that the planning permission could and would determine the number of caravans permitted as a proper planning consideration; site licences involved different considerations, such as hygiene, and might restrict but could not increase the number permitted.

18–105 A draft bill on conversion of ultra-long leases, following the SLC Report, was put out to consultation and the Long Leases (Scotland) Bill was introduced in the Scottish Parliament on November 10, 2010. It sets out an elaborate scheme for the conversion to ownership of the right of a tenant under a registered long lease as defined, in general one for more than 175 years with more than 100 years to run, with various exceptions including mineral leases. It is not intended to apply to commercial leases. Reserved game or fishing rights could be converted into separate tenements (Pt 1). Qualifying leasehold conditions would be converted to real burdens by nomination of a benefited property or by agreement, with possible intervention by the Lands Tribunal for Scotland and with special provision for conversion of personal pre-emption or redemption burdens, economic development burdens, health care burdens, climate change burdens, conservation burdens, facility or service burdens, manager burdens, common scheme burdens and burdens expressly enforceable by third parties, the converted burdens being subject to any counter obligations and obligations assumed by public authorities being excepted (Pt 2). There is elaborate provision for payment of compensation for loss of the landlord's rights (Pt 3). Leases where the tenant registers and does not withdraw an exemption notice are exempt as are leases registered near or after the appointed day (within two years of the first following Whitsunday or Martinmas). See *Conveyancing 2010*, pp.68–69; C. Rae, 2011 Prop. L.B. 110-3. The Justice Committee on March 11, 2011 recommended that the general principles of the Bill be approved but the Bill fell with the dissolution of parliament on March 25, 2011. It is included in the Scottish Government's legislative programme for 2011–2012.

18–108 **fn.474.** *Multilink Leisure Developments Ltd v N. Lanarkshire Council* [2010] CSOH 114; 2009 S.L.T. 1170; reversed [2009] CSIH 46; 2010 S.C. 302; reversal affirmed [2010] UKSC 47; 2011 S.L.T. 184; 2011 U.K.S.C. 53 discussed in *Conveyancing 2010*, pp.35 and 157; G. Junor, "Interpreting the Lease—Without Windfall" (2011) 79 S.L.G. 19; I Doran, "Supreme Court allows "Hope Value" in Land Valuation" 2011 Prop. L.B. 18-108.

18–109 et seq. See *Stair Memorial Encyclopaedia Reissue* "Crofting", paras 58–72 and on the crofting community right to buy paras 73–80.

18–111 **fnn.481 and 485.** The 2010 Crofting Act s.40 (brought into force from July 1, 2011, with savings, by the Commencement Order (SSI 2010/437), arts 3 and

5(1)) inserts subs.(1A) in s.13 of the 1993 Act to provide that for the purposes of subs.(1)(a) only a member of the crofter's family may be the crofter's nominee and s.41 (also brought into force from July 1, 2011 by the same commencement provision, with saving in art.5(2)) in respect of s.14(3) substitutes "ten" for "five"; M.M. Combe, "Crofting, Nominee Sales and the Separation of Powers" (2010) 14 Edin. L.R. 458 discusses the background to the amendments; B. Inkster, "All Change on the Croft" (2011) 56(6) J.L.S. 45.

fn.494. M Combe, "Ruaig an Fhidh ["The Deer Drive"]" (2011) 56(5) J.L.S. **18–115**
54 deals with the attempts of the Pairc Estate crofters to acquire their croft land and an interposed lease and refers to his earlier articles. The owner is challenging s.69A of the 2003 Act.

fn.500. The Pairc Estate case is reported as *Scottish Ministers v Pairc Trust* **18–116**
Ltd, 2007 S.C.L.R. 166.

Under the proposals of the SLC on revision of the land registration system the **18–122**
provisions on acquisition of the landlord's interest by a tenant-at-will contained in the Land Registration (Scotland) Act 1979 would be taken out of the body of the new Land Registration Act and re-enacted in a Schedule.

fn.532. *Wright v Shoreline Management Ltd* is now reported at 2009 S.L.T. (Sh. Ct) 83.

The right to buy is further restricted by the Housing (Scotland) Act 2010, ("the **18–124**
2010 Act"), although s.140, in force from March 1, 2011 by the Commencement Order SSI 2011/96, with a saving provision in art.5, does amend the Housing (Scotland) Act 1987 s.61 to protect the right to buy of tenants re-accommodated where possession has been recovered under various provisions of the Housing (Scotland) Act 2001 or because accommodation was made available by written agreement following a decision to demolish the tenant's house.

Sections 145–147 of the 2010 Act impose duties on the Scottish Ministers to collect and publish relevant information on operation of the right to buy and the sale of houses by registered social landlords but are not yet in force.

(ii) The 2010 Act s.141, brought into force from March 1, 2011 by the **18–125**
Commencement Order SSI 2011/96 noted above, with a transitional provision in art.3, inserts a new s.61ZA into the 1987 Act to limit the right to buy in the case of new tenants, that is, those whose tenancy began on or after s.141 comes into force, i.e. on March 1, 2011, and who had not been in continuous occupation of the premises concerned (as "continuous occupation" is defined in the section, which requires disregard of the period between termination under the Housing (Scotland) Act 2001 ss.18(2), 20(3) or 22(3) and re-accommodation under ss.19(3)(b), 21(3)(b) or 22(6) and allows the landlord to disregard an interruption in occupation which appears to result from circumstances outwith the tenant's control).

The 2010 Act s.143 adds s.61F to the 1987 Act and was brought into force as from January 3, 2011 by the Housing (Scotland) Act 2010 (Commencement No.1) Order 2010 (SSI 2010/444) for the purpose of making regulations on the form of notice required under s.61F(2)(d)—the Limitation on Right to Purchase (Form of Notice) (Scotland) Regulations 2010 (SSI 2010/468), in force from March 1, 2011. Section 61F provides that the 1987 Act s.61 does not in general apply to a "new supply social house", namely, a house let under a Scottish secure tenancy created on or after the day when s.143 came into force, i.e. January 3, 2011, and which was not let under a Scottish secure tenancy on or before June 25, 2008 or acquired by the landlord on or after that date (s.143(3)). There are exceptions set out in s.143(2)(a)–(d), essentially where the tenant is being re-accommodated (cases (a) to (c)) or the landlord has failed to give in due time the notice prescribed by the above Regulations informing the tenant that there is no right to buy (case (d)). Notes to the Regulations inform the tenant of the exceptions and refer to the Scottish Government booklet "Your Right to Buy Your House".

(iii) The 2010 Act s.142, brought into force from June 30, 2011 by the Commencement Order SSI 2011/96, in subs.(1) amends the Housing (Scotland) Act 1987 s.61B to allow local authorities, without consent of the Scottish Ministers as before but in accordance with guidance issued by them (a new s.61C(4) inserted by s.142(2)(c)), to designate any part of their area either generally for all houses or in relation to specified particular types of houses (s.61B(1A) and (1B)) as pressured areas. The designation may last for up to ten years (s.61B(1C)) and there is consequential detailed amendment to s.61(C) (s.142(2)). The designation may be amended or revoked.

fn.564. The Right to Purchase (Application Form) (Scotland) Order 2011 (SSI 2011/97) replaced the 2002 Order as from March 1, 2011.

18–129 The 2010 Act s.144, in force from March 1, 2011 under the Commencement Order SSI 2011/96, inserted a new s.69A into the 1987 Act allowing a local authority to serve a notice of refusal where an application to purchase is served in respect of a house held for the purposes of a police force, having regard to various factors set out in s.69A(3) and (4) relating to police requirements and the circumstances of the tenant. The notice of refusal must contain enough information to demonstrate that the local authority has had regard to the likely impact of the purchase on police operations and resources and any representations by the tenant indicating special reasons for wishing to purchase the house (s.69A(5). There is a saving provision in art.6 of the Order for applications made before March 1, 2011.

18–131 **fn.577.** cf. *Robb v Tayside Joint Police Board (No.3)*, Unreported March 1, 2010, Lands Tr.

18–135 **fn.594.** *Souter v McAuley*, 2010 S.L.T. (Sh.Ct) 121.

18–143 et seq. Under the proposals of the SLC on the revision of the system of land registration there would be specific amendment of the Registration of Leases (Scotland) Act 1857, enacted in a Schedule to the new Land Registration Act, to deal with registered as opposed to recorded leases, instead of relying on the translation provisions of the 1979 Act as at present.

18–148 It is common, especially in residential tenancies, to require from tenants a deposit as security for performance of their obligations. Disputes over wrongful failure by landlords to return deposits in various circumstances are also common and the Housing (Scotland) Act 2006 (asp 1) Pt 4 (ss.120–123), brought into force by the Housing (Scotland) Act 2006 (Commencement No.9) Order (SSI 2010/436) as from December 21, 2010, provides for tenancy deposit schemes (s.120) to safeguard deposits paid in connection with occupation of any living accommodation (whether under a tenancy or an occupancy arrangement). Schemes devised by them or any other person have to be approved by the Scottish Ministers (s.122) under conditions set out in regulations (the Tenancy Deposit Schemes (Scotland) Regulations 2011 (SSI 2011/176)) which also make further provisions on them. Section 123 amends the Rent (Scotland) Act 1984 s.90(3) to insert "for rent" after "obligations" while the Private Rented Housing (Scotland) Act 2011 referred to in para.**18–12** will clarify what charges may legitimately be imposed in connection with grant of a tenancy. Section 32(1) will repeal the words "in addition to the rent" in the Rent (Scotland) Act 1984 s.82(1) and (2); s.32(2) will insert s.89A allowing the Scottish Ministers to make, after due consultation (s.89A(3)) and by statutory instrument a draft of which has been laid before and approved by resolution of the Scottish Parliament (s.89A(4) and (5)), regulations on sums which may be charged in connection with the grant, renewal or continuance of a protected tenancy; s.32(3) and (4) will redefine "premium" in the 1984 Act ss.90(1) and 115(1) to mean any fine, sum or pecuniary consideration, other than the rent, including any service or administration fee or charge

The Private Rented Housing (Scotland) 2011 Act s.33, brought into force from August 31, 2011 by the Commencement Order (SSI 2011/270) to allow the relevant subordinate legislation, will insert in the Housing (Scotland) Act 1988, a new s.30A imposing a duty on landlords to give to tenants under an assured tenancy, no later than the commencement of the tenancy, "standard tenancy documents" as defined in a new s.30B, which gives the Scottish Ministers power, after due consultation (s.30B(2)), to specify them by order, to include information about the tenancy, the house, the landlord, the rights and responsibilities of the parties and copies of any documents which the landlord is under a statutory duty to provide.

A general point potentially affecting all leases is that from April 6, 2011 land agreements will no longer be excluded from the provisions of the Competition Act 1998 and this will affect such matters as use restrictions on competing users in a shopping centre—S. Kerr, "Competition and Land Agreements", 2010 Prop. L.B. 108-3 and A. Wade and A Sharma, "Competition Law and Land Agreements", 2010 Prop. L.B. 109-1; C. Munro, "Land Agreements and the Open Market" (2011) 56(4) J.L.S. 52.

Warren James (Jewellers) Ltd v Overgate G P Ltd [2010] CSOH 57; 2010   **18–152** G.W.D. 17-348, discussed in *Conveyancing 2010*, pp.38 and 184—held that an action for damages for breach of an exclusivity clause in a lease by grant of a competing lease prescribed in five years as, although the obligation related to land, the action was not for enforcement of it but for damages; the breach was not a continuing one but occurred on the grant of the competing lease, applying *A v Glasgow City Council*, 2010 S.L.T. 358.

Tenants of the same landlord may have an interest in seeking to control the   **18–153** purposes for which other neighbouring properties are let—see *Ralph Lauren*   **and 18–** *London Ltd v Trustee of the London Borough of Southwark Pension Fund*   **154** [2011] CSOH 103; 2011 G.W.D. 22-494. The refusal of interim interdict in that case was overturned on appeal on the ground that more debate was needed on the potential application of the relevant provisions of the lease— (2011) 56(7) J.L.S.59.

On crofts see *Stair Memorial Encyclopaedia Reissue* "Crofting", paras 39–42   **18–154** and the Crofting (Scotland) Act 2010 s.33, amending the 1993 Act s.5.

The Antisocial Behaviour (Houses Used for Holiday Purposes) (Scotland) Order 2011 (SSI 2011/201) modifies Pt 7 of the Antisocial Behaviour etc. (Scotland) Act 2004 to enable local authorities to use it to address antisocial behaviour in relation to properties used for holiday purposes, with consequential amendment of the Antisocial Behaviour Notice (Landlord Liability) (Scotland) Regulations 2005 (SSI 2005/562).

18–155   *Geoffrey (Tailor) Highland Crafts Ltd v G L Attractions Ltd*, 2010 G.W.D. 8-142, Sh. Ct—held that limited use was an implied term of the lease, following the opinion of Lord Reed in *Credential Bath St Ltd v Venture Investment Placement Ltd* [2007] CSOH 208 on the construction of the wording of a contract in the light of the factual matrix.

18–156   The provisions of the Disability Discrimination Act 1995 are now contained in the Equality Act 2010 s.189 and Sch.21 with Schs 2 and 4 and s.190 while public authorities are defined in s.150 and Sch.19, with power to add to their number in s.151.

18–159   **fn.692.** I. Doran, "Making Headlines: Rent Reviews Back in the News", 2011 Prop. L.B. 111-2.

18–179   *The Mount Stuart Trust v McCulloch* [2010] CSIH 21; 2010 S.C. 404—held that in case of a rent review under the Agricultural Holdings (Scotland) Act 1991 s.13 the old rent remains due until a determination is made; failure to pay the old rent was in the circumstances a remediable breach of the terms of the lease applying the test of what is remediable in a common-sense way; A.G. Fox and F.M. Stephen, "Courting Controversy" (2010) 55(9) J.L.S. 50.

The Land Court reviewed at length the application of the 1991 Act s.13 in *Morrison-Low v Paterson, SLC/233/08*, June 2, 2010 (the "Moonzie case") commented on by A.G. Fox and F.M. Stephen, "Courting Controversy", above; both parties have appealed.

The Agricultural Holdings Order 2011 art.5 amends the 1991 Act s.13(1) by adding "following notice in writing served on the other party". The promised Agricultural Holdings (Amendment) (Scotland) Bill will prohibit "upward only" and "landlord only" initiated rent reviews and nullify the effect of any decision that the rent includes VAT on rent reviews; C. Clark, "Farm Tenancies: More Changes Imminent" (2011) 56(6) J.L.S. 57.

18–180   *The Colstoun Trust v Firm of A.C. Stoddart & Sons, Colstoun* (1995) [2010] CSIH 20; 2010 S.C. 399—observations on the inherent jurisdiction of the Land Court to regulate its procedure in the absence of a specific rule and on the application of the Agricultural Holdings (Scotland) Act 1991 s.13(8)(b). The Inner House reserved its opinion on dicta that s.13(8)(b) does not apply to a "minimal" resumption and that a rent reduction associated with an agreed resumption constitutes a reduction under s.13(8)(b) and is to be disregarded, observing that the Land Court should be cautious in making obiter dicta on unresolved questions of law.

18–181   The Agricultural Holdings Order 2011 art.4 substitutes a new s.5(4B), qualified by s.5(4BA), in the Agricultural Holdings (Scotland) Act 1991 referring to a date six months before a variation of rent takes effect.

On the rent of crofts see the *Stair Memorial Encyclopaedia Reissue* **18–183**
"Crofting", paras 39–42.

fn.822. The problems arising from deficiencies in the amendments made by the **18–191**
2007 Act and the uncertainties these cause are discussed in A. McAllister, "The
Landlord's Hypothec: Down but is It Out?", 2010 Jur. Rev. 65, pointing out
that as a security right the hypothec raises issues other than sequestration; S.
Skea and A.J.M. Steven, "The Landlord's Hypothec: Difficulties in Practice",
2010 S.L.T. (News) 120.

The case of *Hines v King Sturge LLP* [2010] CSIH 86; 2011 S.L.T. 2 raises the **18–201**
question whether the agent of a landlord owes a duty in delict towards tenants
to avoid damage, in that case by failing to maintain a fire alarm system. A
proof before answer was allowed.

fn.844. G. Jackson, "Energy Performance Certificates and Leases", 2009
Prop. L.B. 99-1.

For a review of the cases on the distinction between ordinary repairs for which **18–202**
a tenant is normally liable and extraordinary repairs for which he is not (unless **and 18–**
the lease provides otherwise) see *Co-operative Insurance Society Ltd v Fife* **210**
Council [2011] CSOH 76; 2011 G.W.D. 19-458, noted by A. Duncan, 2011
Prop. L.R. 113-7; see also *Crieff Highland Gathering Ltd v Perth and Kinross
Council* [2010] CSOH 67 and [2011] CSOH 78; 2011 G.W.D. 20-474 in
para.**18–232** below.

fn.854. On interpretation of a repairing obligation see *Almondvale Investment* **18–202**
(Jersey) Ltd v Technical and General Guarantee Co SA, 2010 G.W.D. 31-651,
Sh. Ct.

On the landlord's liability for repairs under the statutory scheme see A. **18–206**
Stalker, "Todd v Clapperton: The Evolving Law on Repairing Obligations
and Claims against Landlords of Residential Property", 2010 S.L.T. (News)
31.
     The Private Rented Housing (Scotland) Act 2011 s.35(2) will amend the
Housing (Scotland) Act 2006 s.21(3) and (4) to insert references to "the
members of the panel", taking account of the new powers given by the 2011
Act; s.35(3) will give s.22 of the 2006 Act the title "Tenant application to
private rented housing panel"; s.35(4) will insert s.28A in the 2006 Act
entitled "Landlord application to private rented housing panel" allowing a
landlord to apply to the panel for assistance under a new s.28C in exercising
the landlord's right of entry under the 2006 Act s.181(4) to view the state and
condition of the house to see whether it meets the repairing standard and carry
out work necessary to comply with his duty under s.14(1)(b) or a repairing
standard enforcement order. The application, further regulations on the
making or deciding of which may be made by the Scottish Ministers under
s.28B, is allocated by the president of the panel to an individual panel
member to deal with it as provided for in s.28A, e.g. deciding whether to
assist and making necessary arrangements; s.28C provides for arranging a
suitable time for access where it is decided to assist; s.35(5) will add
consequential requirements to the annual report under s.29 and s.35(6)–(8)
will make consequential amendments in ss.181, 182 (on rights of entry) and
191, the last adding subs.(4A) requiring that a draft of regulations under

s.28B, other than those relating to fees, be laid before and approved by resolution of the Scottish Parliament.

On an ejection warrant under the Housing (Scotland) Act 2006 s.38(1) or Sch.5, para.3(1) see the provisions noted in paras **14–23** and **14–25** above.

18–210 **fn.897.** On the distinction between ordinary and extraordinary repairs see *Crieff Highland Gathering Ltd v Perth and Kinross Council* [2010] CSOH 67; 2010 G.W.D. 22-431—proof before answer and after proof [2011] CSOH 78; 2011 G.W.D. 20-474 and paras **18–202** above and **18–232** below.

18–212 The Agricultural Holdings Order 2011 art.9 substitutes for the present Agricultural Holdings (Scotland) Act 2003 s.16(1)–(5), relating to limited duration tenancies, new provisions on the supply and maintenance of fixed equipment by the landlord similar to those in the Agricultural Holdings (Scotland) Act 1991 s.5, leaving s.16(6) and (7) which nullify agreements shifting responsibility for the landlord's obligations to the tenant. The provisions, which do not differ from the draft, are criticised in detail by A. Fox and D. Reid, "Lacuna Manufacturing—A Commentary on art.9 of the draft Public Services Reform (Agricultural Holdings) (Scotland) Order 2011" (2011) 56(3) J.L.S. 46, observing that the Order is a missed opportunity to clarify agricultural law which badly needs clarification.

18–216 A.G. Fox, "Tackling Improvements" (2009) 54(12) J.L.S. 46—commenting on *R. and M. Whiteford v Trs of Cowhill Trust, Application RN SLC/174/08.*

18–221, 222 and 227 On compensation for improvements and compensation for deterioration of crofts see *Stair Memorial Encyclopaedia Reissue* "Crofting", paras 114–120 and also for provisions on cottars, paras 134–137.

18–230 On a claim by a landlord against administrators for payments under a lease as an expense of administration under the Insolvency Act 1986 see *Cheshire West and Chester Borough Council, Petitioners* [2010] CSOH 115; 2010 G.W.D. 33-684 and article by A.S. Burrows, "Expensive Business" (2010) 55(10) J.L.S. 47.

18–232 On the distinction between ordinary and extraordinary repairs see *Co-operative Insurance Society Ltd v Fife Council* [2011] CSOH 76 and *Crieff Highland Gathering Ltd v Perth and Kinross Council* [2010] CSOH 67; 2010 G.W.D. 22-431 and [2011] CSOH 78; 2011 G.W.D. 20-474.

18–233 The Arbitration (Scotland) Act 2010, brought partly into force by the Arbitration (Scotland) Act 2010 (Commencement No.1 and Transitional Provisions) Order (SSI 2010/195) and supplemented by the Arbitral Appointments Referee (Scotland) Order (SSI 2010/196) and the Arbitration (Scotland) Act 2010 (Consequential Amendments) Order 2010 (SSI 2010/220) does not as yet apply to statutory arbitrations but may apply by agreement.

fn.983. See the special case stated by the Land Court *Jardine v Murray* [2011] CSIH 60.

18–234 In relation to removing it is now necessary to have regard to the provisions noted in paras 14–23 and 14–25 above which apply to removing generally, including removing from residential property, orders for possession under the

Rent (Scotland) Act 1984 s.115(1) and removing and ejection under the Agricultural Holdings (Scotland) Act 2003 s.84(1)(e). In *Capacity Building Project v Edinburgh City Council* [2011] CSOH 58; 2011 G.W.D. 16-395 it was argued unsuccessfully that the Council had no power to terminate a lease of a community centre.

fn.987. On apparent failure of the police to recognise the relevance of the Rent Act 1984 s.22 to incidents of eviction or harassment of tenants see L. Barrie and L. Paterson, "Only a Civil Matter?" (2010) 55(11) J.L.S. 9.

Cases alleging negligence by solicitors in relation to drafting leases—*Legal* **18–237** *Services Centre Ltd v Miller Samuel LLP* [2009] CSOH 141; 2009 G.W.D. 36-616—rent review clause; *Credential Bath Street Ltd v DLA Piper Scotland LLP* [2010] CSOH 26; 2010 G.W.D. 17-347—drafting and enforcement of guarantee of obligations of tenant; R. Rennie, "Solicitors' Negligence—New Developments", 2010 S.L.T. (News) 159.

INDEX

Please note: the paragraph numbers reference those of the main publication, *Scottish Land Law*, Vol.I.